Technology-Enhance
Learning of Chinese as a Foreign Language

Technology-Enhanced Teaching and Learning of Chinese as a Foreign Language provides new and experienced teachers of Chinese with a timely review and evaluation of the use of technology in the language classroom.

The book draws from second language acquisition theories and empirical studies to demonstrate the use of technologies in facilitating language learning. With a strong practical and pedagogical focus, this is an ideal resource for current and prospective teachers of Chinese as a Foreign Language.

Key features include:

- Demonstration and analysis of technologies in use
- Principles and methods to evaluate instructional technologies
- Summary tables presenting the key functions of each technology tool

Online resources include up-to-date information on new technologies and tools to address the ever-changing nature of the topic.

Amber Navarre is Senior Lecturer and former Head of the Chinese Program at Boston University. She specializes in second language acquisition, computer-assisted language learning, and curriculum design. She has won the Gitner Award for Innovation in Teaching with Technology and the international Blackboard Exemplary Course Award.

Routledge Chinese Language Pedagogy
Series Editor: Yongcan Liu

The Routledge Advanced Language Training Course for K-16 Non-native Chinese Teachers
Hong Gang Jin, Lian Xue, Yusheng Yang and Lan Zhao Zhou

Teaching and Learning Chinese in Higher Education
Theoretical and Practical Issues
Yang Lu

Manual for Teaching and Learning Chinese as a Foreign Language
Bo Hu

Technology-Enhanced Teaching and Learning of Chinese as a Foreign Language
Amber Navarre

For more information about this series, please visit: www.routledge.com/Routledge-Chinese-Language-Pedagogy/book-series/RCLP

Technology-Enhanced Teaching and Learning of Chinese as a Foreign Language

Amber Navarre

Routledge
Taylor & Francis Group

LONDON AND NEW YORK

First published 2019
by Routledge
2 Park Square, Milton Park, Abingdon, Oxon OX14 4RN

and by Routledge
711 Third Avenue, New York, NY 10017

Routledge is an imprint of the Taylor & Francis Group, an informa business

British Library Cataloguing in Publication Data
A catalogue record for this book is available from the British Library

Library of Congress Cataloging in Publication Data
A catalog record for this book has been requested

ISBN: 978-1-138-18859-4 (hbk)
ISBN: 978-1-138-18860-0 (pbk)
ISBN: 978-1-315-64221-5 (ebk)

Typeset in Times New Roman
by Out of House Publishing

Visit the eResources: www.routledge.com/9781138188600

Contents

Figures

Tables

How to use this book

I write this book to help current and prospective Chinese teachers to explore, assess, and implement instructional technologies to facilitate learning. Through the chapters, I invite my reader-teachers to reflect on their own use and come up with plans for future integration of technology in light of second language acquisition (SLA) theories and empirical studies, foreign language standards, and principles for best practices in the field.

Chapter 1 and 2 are overarching chapters discussing why and how language teachers use technology in their design of learning experiences. Chapter 1 provides an overview of the utilization of instructional technology in foreign language education and discusses the relationship between instructional technology integration and teacher beliefs. Chapter 2 maps out important factors to consider when assessing and integrating technologies into the curriculum.

Chapter 3 serves as a bridge between SLA theories and practices, discussing the areas where technologies may be of service in the learning process. Starting with this chapter, a wide variety of technological tools and techniques will be introduced in each chapter, with examples drawn from master teachers' classes in both K-12 and postsecondary levels.

Chapter 4, 5, and 6 are "practical guide" chapters, in which I introduce hundreds of technological tools and techniques that benefit Chinese learners in developing proficiency and help teachers to design learner-centered learning experiences. I would strongly recommend my readers to apply the principles introduced earlier in Chapter 2 when exploring the tools and techniques introduced in these chapters in order to choose the ones that best suit their learners' needs.

Recognizing that technology develops and changes rapidly and that even with the hundreds of tools introduced, this book cannot possibly cover all currently available technologies, let alone the ones to come after its publication, Chapter 7 concludes the book by pointing to online resources and aims to equip my reader-teachers with the mindsets and methods that help them to explore and research emerging instructional technologies independently.

For quick referencing, I include lists of mentioned resources and tools at the end of each chapter, from Chapter 3 to Chapter 7. Resources refer to those that provide content (e.g., reading/listening materials; information for teachers); tools on the other hand are services or applications that require teachers or learners to actively operate and produce their own content. For each tool, a table is provided, which includes its name, function, difficulty level, and product website for easy access. Please note in regard to the difficulty level of each tool:

1. The difficulty level is based on how easy it is for the teacher to operate it. For instance, a service that collects learners' speech input might only require the learner to click a button and record, but the teacher has to learn how to input and arrange the prompts, adjust display settings, share the assignment, and access and provide feedback to each learner's recording on the platform. My scoring of difficulty level is based on the latter.
2. When it comes to selecting tools, it is not necessarily the case that easier is better. While tools of lower difficulty level are indeed easier for the teacher to operate, tools of higher difficulty levels tend to have more sophisticated functions or more customized options to choose from. Similarly, it is also not true that more advanced functions/options are always better, as they may or may not add to the targeted learning outcomes. If the preferred learning outcomes can be achieved with an easy tool, by all means use it and save yourself the time and effort. On the other hand, if the learning experience and effect may be improved by a more complicated tool, you may want to consider investing time and energy on learning it, as long as it is within your level of learnability and comfort.

During the two years I was writing this book, the biggest challenge for me was the quick turnover of technologies. We bid farewell to many once-beloved services, such as Zaption in 2016, Movie Maker in 2017, and Wikispace to be discontinued in 2018. In the meantime, new tools and services keep emerging and entering the realm of foreign language education, such as the launch of Adobe Sparks and Story Remix in 2017, in addition to the constant updates and expansions developed within already existent programs. I have strived to find replacements for the services that ceased to exist and keep the information of this book updated with new technological developments. However, the fast-evolving nature of technology almost guarantees that between the time I finish this book and the time you read it, some changes may have occurred and made the information less than 100% up to date. I apologize if it happens and sincerely hope the tips I provide in the book help you become a more competent and confident user of instructional technologies, who explores both independently and collaboratively with other teachers beyond the limits of the current book.

1 The drives

What is behind our decisions regarding instructional technology?

In this century, teaching without using any technology has become almost literally impossible. From using overhead projectors to present slides, to posting student grades on the course management system, to answering students' questions via email, to adopting online textbooks and other materials, to having students look up information on search engines, to incorporating social media and building a learning community, to delegating some learning activities to the online environment or offering the whole course online, this list goes on and expands day by day. Every school, every class, every teacher, and every student are expected to use technology to varying degrees. As stated in the most recent National Education Technology Plan by the U.S. Department of Education (2016), "the conversation has shifted from *whether* technology should be used in learning to *how* it can improve learning to ensure that all students have access to high-quality educational experiences" (p. 5).

How to use technology to improve learning experiences in a Chinese language classroom is exactly the focus of this book. But before we get into the practical planning, selection, and use of technology, let's take a minute to think about *why* we want to incorporate technology in our teaching. As the social critic Paul Goodman (1970) wrote in reaction to the quickly emerging technology half a century ago, "whether or not it draws on new scientific research, technology is a branch of moral philosophy, not of science" (p. 40). Whether technology itself is a branch of moral philosophy or science is open to further discussion among scholars, but it is nevertheless true that the way we choose to incorporate technology into our teaching is driven by our philosophy of technology. Just like how our teaching philosophy governs what we decide to teach and how we teach it, our beliefs, attitudes, motivations, and knowledge in regard to the relationship between technology and education construe the answer as to how we use technology in our teaching.

Why do we use technology? There are many good reasons to do so according to thousands of studies. For instance:

Technology increases the accessibility of learning materials and expands learning experiences

Technology increases learners' access to foreign language education in many ways.

For those who take face-to-face language courses in schools, the Internet allows them exposure to authentic target language materials through webpages, blogs, forums, streamed videos, and social media. Teachers who teach less commonly taught languages may find such online resources particularly helpful because the authentic materials are otherwise hard to find.

Sometimes schools might not be able to offer face-to-face courses of certain languages to interested students due to low enrollment or difficulty in finding certified teachers, especially in the cases of less commonly taught languages and more rural districts. These interested learners may now access such courses through virtual classrooms. In the case of Chinese, online courses are often offered by individual universities at the level of higher education, while K-12 courses are often offered by virtual classroom services in collaboration with educational organizations who have expertise in language education. For instance, Michigan Virtual School collaborates with the Confucius Institute at Michigan State University (CI-MSU); K12.com, the biggest education management organization (EMO) in the United States, offers their Chinese courses through Middlebury College's Interactive Languages.

In addition to increased access to learning materials and resources, students who enroll in a face-to-face program may also expand their learning experience beyond the classroom with the help of technology. Teachers may assign students to conduct research by finding information online about the target culture or have them do group projects via virtual collaboration. Some schools have virtual dual language programs or less formal exchanges (e.g., a shared blog, key-pal partnership, or periodical virtual conferences) with students from a collaborative foreign institute. In a flipped classroom, which we will discuss further in Chapter 6, instruction is frequently digitally recorded and viewed by learners at home. All these learning experiences beyond the classroom increase the contact hours with the target language, which is recognized as crucial for learning a foreign language, especially Category IV languages,[1] including Chinese.

Technology helps to tailor learning experiences to individual learners' needs

Technology can make it easier for teachers to design learning experiences that appeal to learners' different proficiency levels, learning styles, and emotional or social needs. For instance, using multimedia materials allows learners to have both visual and audio input at the same time; having course content available online allows learners to (re)learn the lesson at their own pace; doing multimedia projects such as digital storytelling or film/animation production encourages learners to use the target language meaningfully, collaboratively, and creatively.

Many studies have pointed out that communication in a second language in an e-learning environment is less stressful or threatening to learners than face-to-face settings (e.g., Chun, 1998; Casanave, 2004; Rubesch & McNeil, 2010; Huang & Hwang, 2013).

Technology enables quick feedback and more variety when assessing learners' performance

Compared to paper-based assessments, technology-assisted assessments have been found to be more efficient by reducing the time, resources, and disruption to learning (Gohl, Gohl, & Wolf, 2009). One major advantage of using technology to assess learning is that it enables quick feedback, which is particularly useful in the case of formative assessments. With the current polling/quizzing tools, teachers may embed assessment questions within the lesson, conduct comprehension checks in an undisruptive manner, receive immediate feedback, and quickly adjust their lesson plan to address the content students struggle with. Individual learners may also receive immediate feedback and know where they stand in the learning process. With their progress being transparent to the learners, they may take more autonomy and decide their next step of learning. In other words, the teacher and the learners jointly shape the learning experience and fine-tune it constantly based on the quick feedback gained through technology.

Furthermore, in a language classroom, assessment should not be and has never been limited to paper tests and quick quizzing/polling. Technology may also help provide variety while assessing a wide array of communication in different modes and with different tasks. For instance, authentic multimedia materials may be used to assess listening and reading comprehension; audio/video recording may be used to assess interpersonal and presentational modes of speaking; a real-life problem-solving project may be used for an integrated assessment that involves multiple language skills, cultural knowledge, and communication modes, such as finding and presenting the most appropriate lodging arrangement when traveling in China by comparing options online. Technology did not invent such assessment methods but has enabled a wider variety of tasks learners may undertake to demonstrate learning.

Technology facilitates collaboration and formation of learner communities

Technology helps facilitate collaboration in many ways. First of all, for learners, technology helps transcend the limitation of time and space, allowing them to collaborate on projects beyond school hours and settings. Learners may work together outside of the classroom synchronously using video-conferencing tools (e.g., Skype, Google Hangout, or Zoom) and real-time editing applications (e.g., Google Docs or Microsoft Word Online), or asynchronously via email or text messaging.

Many teachers host course blogs, micro-blogs (e.g., Twitter or Weibo), wikis, or social media groups to share course content, events, resources, thoughts, and opinions with students, parents, and even local and global communities. For instance, some study abroad programs ask students to keep a reflection journal on their blogs about their experiences. These blogs are not only the platform for learners to reflect on their intercultural learning, but also serve as the site for parents to witness or actively participate in their learning by viewing and commenting (Kelm, 2011; Lee, 2011; Jin, 2012).

While it is not required for learners to share their video or audio projects publicly, many choose to do so and broadcast their projects to a general audience and reach out to the global community. For instance, a keyword search of "Chinese student project" on YouTube would generate thousands of results.

Teachers may also take advantage of collaborative technology among themselves to share resources and lesson plans, ask questions, provide support, and work on cross-institute or interdisciplinary projects together (Lord & Lomicka, 2004; Arnold, Ducate, Lomicka, & Lord, 2005; Arnold & Ducate, 2006). Such virtual collaboration may be even more important for teachers who are the only teacher of the subject in their school or school district, which is a common situation for Chinese teachers. Over the Internet, these teachers may communicate, share, and work with one another remotely via virtual collaboration.

Technology encourages self-learning and lifelong learning

One ultimate goal of education is to cultivate lifelong learners who would continue to learn: to acquire resources, think critically, and use the learned knowledge and skills to solve real-life problems beyond formal school settings. Demand for *knowledge workers*, who are educated and able to continuously update their knowledge, presents the driving force for educational policy makers and institutions to transform the current education system to one that cultivates such lifelong learners (Evers, Rush, & Berdrow, 1998; Rowley, Lujan, & Dolence, 1998). A key to continuous lifelong learning lies in the dynamic large-scale online communities that provide indefinite learning resources and attract active users/contributors worldwide (Thomas & Brown, 2011), which is what our education should prepare and guide young learners to explore. Information or technology literacy is included in most lists that aim to define the twenty-first-century skills for learners at both national (e.g., Framework for 21st Century Learning; Assessment and Teaching of 21st Century Skills; Common Core State Standards) and local levels (e.g., Iowa Essential Concepts and Skills; Connecticut's Common Core of Learning; Illinois Learning Standards).

The cultivation of lifelong learners is crucial for language learning, arguably more than other subjects, since the mastery of the subject may not be achieved without immersing oneself in authentic language environments outside of the classroom. Given the required hours for learning a foreign language, especially a Category IV language such as Chinese, the pursuit of mastery may last well beyond the learner's school years. Therefore, an important mission for us teachers is to prepare our learners with the skills and attitudes ready for lifelong learning when they are out of our classes.

Lifelong learning requires both autonomy and collaboration, and technology may help prepare learners for both. On the one hand, technology increases the accessibility to learning materials and expands learning experiences beyond the classroom. With mobile devices in the picture, the language learning experience could be literally seamless and ubiquitous. Learners may watch a video, listen to lesson recordings, use flashcards, or even practice writing on their phone or tablets anywhere, anytime. When they encounter a problem, instead of waiting to ask the teacher the next day in school, they may look it up online, or post their questions and get answers from a virtual community. Such learning is by nature self-purposed, self-directed, and self-paced. Guiding learners to use such resources in a language class may help develop the mindset and familiarize them with the methods for such independent learning.

On the other hand, language classes may also help to cultivate lifelong learners through promoting virtual communication and collaboration so that learners may participate in the larger community of the target language and culture and continue with their learning. Analyzing the language use on authentic websites, blogs, and forums may help learners learn to evaluate the text in its social context and develop critical thinking skills. On the social level, having students communicate in a controlled social platform, such as a closed Facebook group or a private course blog, would allow them to practice developing a virtual identity and using appropriate language and/or *netiquette* (Internet etiquette) while interacting with others in a relatively safe online environment with the teacher's guidance and monitoring.

While the reasons mentioned above are great ones to incorporate technology in our teaching, the benefits of using technology are not the only reasons teachers use it. In addition to these benefits technology brings to learning, which *pull* many teachers to use technology in their classes, there are also *pushing* forces for teachers to abandon traditional non-technology teaching, one of which is the pressure coming from the general climate or the teacher's immediate environment.

In general, the importance of technology is often stressed in education policies and made relevant to the social changes and economic growth at national and international level. For instance, acknowledging that "societal and economic potential can come from harnessing technological innovation in higher education," Androulla Vassiliou, the then European Commissioner for Education, Culture, Multilingualism and Youth, urged that "it is imperative that Europe takes the lead in this area" (European Commission, 2014, p. 4) in the report to the European Commission on new modes of learning and teaching in higher education. It is also predicted in the report that by 2024, e-learning may grow fifteen-fold in Europe and "with the promise, or threat, the digital technology will revolutionise our traditional, bricks and mortar universities" (p. 6). In the United States, technology is mentioned more than 100 times in the Common Core State Standards, and "similar expectations exist in states adopting other college- and career-ready standards." (U.S. Department of Education, 2016, p. 32).

While the incorporation of technology is viewed as a sign of educational progress or superiority, the direct impact of such policies is that the performance of schools and universities are evaluated accordingly, which causes school administrators to look for the use of technology as evidence of effective teaching. Such emphasis on the technological competence of teachers is reflected on the job market. Just glancing over the first page of job postings on the website of the Chinese Language Teachers Association, the biggest job board for Chinese teachers in the United States, requirements such as "skills in effective use of pedagogical technology" (University of Iowa, IA), "comfortable working with technology" (Peninsula High School, WA), "experience in technology-based Chinese L2 instruction and courseware design" (West Kentucky University, KY), "oversee website design and content" (University of Rhode Island, RI), "knowledge of a variety of contemporary teaching approaches and language learning technologies" (George Washington University, DC), "familiarity with current methods and technologies in foreign language teaching" (Pennsylvania State University, PA), "experience with online learning" (Middlebury Interactive Languages, DE), and "skilled in the use of educational technology in the service of learning" (Chinese American International School, CA) popped up (search conducted on July 18, 2016).

Under the pressure that their (continuous) employment at least partially depends on successful incorporation of technology in their classes, language teachers may attempt technology integration regardless of whether they recognize the aforementioned educational benefits brought about by technology. However, while behavior-wise most teachers do use technology in their classes, the different motivations teachers have for using technology (i.e., for the various learning benefits vis-à-vis for the purpose of employment) still strongly impact how much and how effectively they incorporate technology in their teaching (Ertmer et al., 1999; Baylor & Ritchie, 2002; Meskill, Mossop, DiAngelo, & Pasquale, 2002; Ertmer, 2005).

The spectrum of teachers' attitudes towards technology utilization may be roughly divided into four categories: To one end there are conservatives and to the other enthusiasts, and between them there are skeptical and curious users:

> *The conservatives* are those who do not believe in any learning and managerial benefits technology may bring to their classes. We may hear

them say (with pride) that a good teacher can teach well without technology. They view technology as a distraction and impediment to learning and typically dread or despise learning new tools. Their incorporation of technology tends to be minimal.

The skeptical users do use *some* technology in their classes but often for the sake of school requirement, continuous employment, or peer pressure. They remain skeptical about the benefits of instructional technology and are at best lukewarm about learning new tools.

The curious users view technology as having considerable potential to improve their teaching and tend to actively seek training in order to harness this potential. They might not have incorporated a lot of technology in their classes yet, mostly because of lack of competence, practice, or confidence, but they are eager to learn new tools and model after other teachers who are more experienced in this area.

The enthusiasts believe in the transformative power of technology in education. They do not hesitate to try and experiment with new tools in their classes. Many of them actively participate in online communities and follow the news about emerging tools. Some of them might even take part in designing new tools. They tend to use technology creatively, not only with tools designed for educational purposes, but also adapting general tools for learning contexts. Because the enthusiasts strive to update themselves with the ever-changing technology, they tend to become the experts in their program/school/field that other teachers turn to for help and advice.

If you identify with the conservatives or skeptical users, I am pleasantly surprised that you are reading this book. I humbly hope this book will help you open up more to the potential benefits technology may bring to you and your learners. I also hope that by seeing how other teachers incorporate easy-to-use technology in this book you may gain more confidence and become more open to trying some tools in your own classes. As Meskill and colleagues (2002) pointed out, it is not just knowing how to use technology but the combination of training and the actual experience of using it in one's classroom that makes a teacher comfortable with using technology.

If you are a curious user, I would like to say that I have written this book mostly for you. According to European Commission's report (2014), two-thirds of current higher education teachers recognize that technology may benefit their teaching, but half of them reported that they need training to actually incorporate more technology in their classes. Since Chinese teachers tend to work in isolation and might not have master teachers to model after or training workshops to attend in their immediate teaching environment, this book aims to fill this gap by providing guidelines for choosing among technologies in Chapter 2 and demonstrating from Chapter 3 to Chapter 6 what learning activities master teachers have designed using technology. I hope this book can help curious teachers gain confidence and inspiration in integrating technology in their own classes.

If you are an enthusiast of technology integration, I hope this book encourages you to reflect deeply on your use of technology in light of pedagogical theories and principles. It is one of the major points that the newest U.S. National Education Technology Plan (U.S. Department of Education, 2016) stressed, compared to the previous version, that teaching transcends technology. As someone who embraces the opportunities and potentials new technology brings, you may sometimes be dazzled by the novelty of newly emerging tools and confuse this novelty for effectiveness in promoting learning, or confuse the *interest* of learners for the real *effect* of learning. To avoid the common myth among enthusiasts that *the more/newer the better*, we need to apply careful assessment of technological tools and practices using language learning standards that focus on teaching and learning experiences rather than the technologies themselves. We will discuss the standards and this process of assessing technologies in the next chapter.

Note

1 The Foreign Service Institute has created a list to rank languages based on their difficulty of learning to native English speakers. (www.state.gov/m/fsi/sls/c78549. htm) Category IV languages include Arabic, Chinese (Mandarin and Cantonese), Japanese, and Korean. The estimated number of hours needed to reach professional proficiency in speaking is 2,200 hours for Category IV.

References

Arnold, N., & Ducate, L. (2006). Future foreign language teachers' social and cognitive collaboration in an online environment. *Language Learning and Technology, 10*(1), 42–66.

Arnold, N., Ducate, L., Lomicka, L., & Lord, G. (2005). Using computer-mediated communication to establish social and supportive environments in teacher education. *CALICO Journal, 22*(3), 537–566.

Baylor, A. L., & Ritchie, D. (2002). What factors facilitate teacher skill, teacher morale, and perceived student learning in technology-using classrooms? *Computers & Education, 39*(4), 395–414.

Casanave, C. P. (2004). *Controversies in second language writing: Dilemmas and decisions in research and instruction.* Ann Arbor, MI: University of Michigan Press.

Chun, D. M. (1998). Using computer-assisted class discussion to facilitate the acquisition of interactive competence. *Language Learning Online: Theory and Practice in the ESL and L2 computer classroom*, 57–80.

Ertmer, P. A. (2005). Teacher pedagogical beliefs: The final frontier in our quest for technology integration? *Educational Technology Research and Development, 53*(4), 25–39.

Ertmer, P. A., Paul, A., Molly, L., Eva, R., & Denise, W. (1999). Examining teachers' beliefs about the role of technology in the elementary classroom. *Journal of Research on Computing in Education, 32*(1), 54–72.

European Commission (2014). *Modernisation of higher education: Report to the European Commission on new modes of learning and teaching in higher education.* Luxembourg: Publications Office of the European Union.

Evers, F. T., Rush, J. C., & Berdrow, I. (1998). *The bases of competence: Skills for life-long learning and employability.* San Francisco, CA: Jossey-Bass.

Gohl, E. M., Gohl, D., & Wolf, M. A. (2009). Assessments and technology: A powerful combination for improving teaching and learning. In L. M. Pinkus (Ed.), *Meaningful measurement: The role of assessments in improving high school education in the twenty-first century* (pp. 183–197). Washington, DC: Alliance for Excellent Education.

Goodman, P. (1970). *New reformation: Notes of a neolithic conservative.* New York: Random House.

Huang, P., & Hwang, Y. (2013). An exploration of EFL learners' anxiety and e-learning environments. *Journal of Language Teaching and Research, 4*(1), 27–35.

Jin, L. (2012). When in China, do as the Chinese do? Learning compliment responding in a study abroad program. *Chinese as a Second Language Research, 1*(2), 211–240.

Kelm, O. R. (2011). Social media: It's what students do. *Business Communication Quarterly, 74*(4), 505–520.

Lee, L. (2011). Blogging: Promoting learner autonomy and intercultural competence through study abroad. *Language Learning & Technology, 15*(3), 87–109.

Lord, G., & Lomicka, L. L. (2004). Developing collaborative cyber communities to prepare tomorrow's teachers. *Foreign Language Annals, 37*(3), 401–408.

Meskill, C., Mossop, J., DiAngelo, S., & Pasquale, R. K. (2002). Expert and novice teachers talking technology: Precepts, concepts, and misconcepts. *Language Learning & Technology, 6*(3), 46–57.

Rowley, D. J., Lujan, H. D., & Dolence, M. G. (1998). *Strategic choices for the academy: How demand for lifelong learning will re-create higher education.* San Francisco, CA: Jossey-Bass Publishers.

Rubesch, T., & McNeil, M. (2010). Online versus face-to-face: Motivating and demotivating factors in an EAP writing course. *The JALT CALL Journal, 6*(3), 235–250.

Thomas, D., & Brown, J. S. (2011). *A new culture of learning: Cultivating the imagination for a world of constant change.* Lexington, KY: CreateSpace.

U.S. Department of Education (2016). *Future ready learning: Reimagining the role of technology in education. 2016 National Education Technology Plan.* Washington, DC: U.S. Department of Education, Office of Educational Technology.

2 The filters

Standards, principles, and considerations for selecting and using instructional technology

A shift in the field of education has occurred in the first decades of the twenty-first century in terms of how instructional technology is viewed and utilized. Such a shift may be well demonstrated by the change of tone from the U.S. National Education Technology Plan (NETP) 2010 to NETP 2016. In NETP 2010, technology was brought to the foreground as a "driver of change" that demanded our commitment to "enable transforming education" (U.S. Department of Education, 2010, p. 4). At the turn of the century, technology was assumed to be the leading force to empower learning and transform teaching. A major problem with this dominant discourse was that such over-enthusiasm may prevent the use of technology from being critically examined. Taking the use of technology as a sign of educational progress or superiority, school administrators and teachers adopted new tools and services, sometimes to the extent that it was done blindly and competitively. The most recent NETP 2016 addressed this potential pitfall and brought teaching and the learning experience back to the center of technology utilization. While recognizing that "*when carefully designed and thoughtfully applied*, technology can accelerate, amplify, and expand the impact of effective teaching practice" (U.S. Department of Education, 2016, p. 3, emphasis added), NETP 2016 reminded the users that "learning principles transcend specific technologies" (ibid, p. 10). Taking this reminder to heart, this chapter will discuss the "filters," namely, the standards, principles, and considerations to help Chinese language teachers to *carefully design and thoughtfully apply* technology, and we will start with the overarching principles of learning and teaching.

Filter 1: The learner

Since our ultimate goal is for learners to learn the language, the *learner* should be at the center of our instructional design and be given the first and utmost consideration when we make decisions regarding technological implementation. Therefore, the first filter I recommend that teachers apply when planning for technological integration would be the learners' language proficiency. There are two major frameworks of proficiency that are commonly referenced to guide the learning, teaching, and assessment of foreign languages, namely, the Proficiency Guidelines developed by the American Council on the Teaching of Foreign Languages (ACTFL, 2012) and the Common European Framework of Reference for Languages (Council of Europe, 2009). A companion volume was added to the latter in 2017 to elaborate the key notions and update illustrative descriptors of CEFR (Council of Europe, 2017).

While it is not the focus of this book to introduce in detail what each proficiency level looks like, it is important for language teachers to carefully examine where their learners' proficiency stands and what they are capable of learning next. An effective lesson should target solidifying the current proficiency level and scaffold the learners to progress into the next, for which you may choose to use technology to help access appropriate materials and create meaningful tasks. Both frameworks are free to download on their official websites. I recommend teachers read through the descriptions and exemplars in these documents to have a general idea about your own learners' current proficiency when thinking about integrating technology into your curriculum. If you are interested in assessing proficiency more precisely and accurately, there are also workshops available for training examiners.

In addition to the learners' language proficiency, their level of technology proficiency is an important factor to consider. Being called "digital natives" (Prensky, 2001), the millennial learners are described as living lives immersed in technology, surrounded by "toys and tools of the digital age" (ibid, p. 1). I have asked the question "What would you do if you encounter a problem with technology when you teach?" many times in the teacher training workshops I have led and "Ask students to help" is one response I receive almost every time. However, the general familiarity with technology among the current generation of learners does not mean that *every* student in your classroom knows how to operate the digital tools you choose or are able to "just figure it out" simply because they were born and raised in a technology-rich environment. As a matter of fact, many studies have pointed out that the use of computers and the Internet among school-aged children, teenagers, and young adults is unevenly spread based on their age, school and home environments, and social backgrounds (Downes, 2002; Lee, 2005; Koivusilta, Lintonen, & Rimpelä, 2007). They also tend to limit themselves to certain functions such as emailing, word processing, and surfing the Internet for pleasure, and only a minority of them publish their own content to the web or engage in exploring emerging technologies (Kvavik, Caruso, & Morgan, 2004; Oliver & Goerke, 2007; Kennedy et al., 2008; Lenhart, Purcell, Smith, & Zickuhr, 2010).

Assessing what our learners are capable of and providing them training in tools with which they are not yet familiar are thus necessary steps before assigning them to work with technology. The assessment of learners' level of competence and comfort in using certain technologies tends to be informal. Instead of running a test on students' actual skills, most teachers simply conduct a poll or use a self-report checklist to find out whether the learners are ready to use a specific technology. In terms of training, some teachers choose to run general orientation sessions with the whole class, such as modeling and demonstration during class or having students do their first project in a teacher-supervised context, while others choose to do differentiated assistance, such as posting step-by-step screen-shot manuals on their course websites as a reference or offering need-based consultation to small groups or individual students outside of class hours. Many technological tools now have tutorial videos available online that can be referred to students who need more guidance as well. No matter whether you choose to do general or differentiated training, it should have a relatively low demand of time and effort for the students to learn to use the chosen technology. If you find it taking a long time or too much effort, it might be a sign of a mismatch between the technology and your students' proficiency. With the millions of tools available in the market, it is highly likely that you may find something that provides similar functions but is easier to operate. To make the process even easier, search or ask questions in language teachers' networks—someone may have found a great solution to your problem already.

Age is another factor to consider when choosing appropriate technologies for your learners. Learners of different ages have different cognitive abilities, different emotional, social, and developmental needs, and different areas of interest. Therefore, the same technology may be received differently by different age groups. For instance, the National Association for the Education of Young Children (NAEYC) published on their website a document called *Selected Examples of Effective Classroom Practice Involving Technology Tools and Interactive Media*, which differentiated the appropriate use of technology and media into three major groups: infants and toddlers, preschoolers and kindergarteners, and school-age children. Curtain and Dahlberg (2010) collected detailed observations from language teachers describing the characteristics of learners in each grade. Although these observations were not made in light of technology integration per se, the association may be easily made to technology tools and tasks appropriate for each grade. For instance, a teacher mentioned their first-graders liked to "take things home, tell endlessly about themselves, move, make things (crafts), draw, and label" (p. 20). From this observation, we may infer that in using tools for digital storytelling, which we will discuss more in detail in Chapter 6, drawing and moving objects on a tablet or an interactive whiteboard would be appropriate. On the other hand, eighth-graders, which were described by another teacher as focusing on "school and peers" and wanting to "learn things and share with their peers in an 'informal' setting" (p. 28, emphasis in original), would probably be more interested in exploring the school life in the target language culture via the Internet, communicating with peers abroad via teleconferencing or social media, and working on collaborative projects such as a group presentation or skit using multimedia.

Learners are different not just as cohorts. There are also individual differences in play. Technology may make it easier to address such individual differences. First of all, technology allows us to present materials to our learners through audio and visual input and interactive exercises to accommodate different learning styles. Similarly, technology enables choices from the learner's side to demonstrate learning evidence. As teachers, we need to make sure we allow for such choices by giving our students not only different tasks, but different *types* of tasks. Choices may even be embedded within one task, such as doing a project individually or with a partner, doing a live or recorded performance, or introducing one's family as a voiceover photo stream, an animated cartoon, or even as a song and musical video. The last example came from a personal experience with my students. When they were asked to introduce their family members and I was explaining to them what formats this project could take, "can I do it as a song?" a student asked. "Of course you can. How about making it a musical video?" I challenged him, and it turned out to be a very creative and fun project. One thing to keep in mind when allowing such flexibility is that all work should address the same learning objectives and can be evaluated by the same criteria.

Filter 2: The design

Placing the learner at the center of instruction, the role of the teacher has shifted from the lecturer of content to the *designer* of learning experiences. As a joint project of the Partnership for 21st Century Learning (P21) and ACTFL, *the 21st Century Skills Map* (Partnership for 21st Century Learning, 2011) compares what the language classroom was like in the past and today (see Table 2.1).

Backward design, as mentioned in Table 2.1, is a commonly used design for planning language curriculum and is adopted by both ACTFL and CEFR. Although the latter states that it is not associated with any specific methods or approaches, the standards-based teaching practice it describes is believed to reflect the principles of backward design (Richards, 2013). The concept of backward design was introduced to the field of curriculum design by Wiggins and McTighe (2005) and included three stages:

Stage 1: Identify desired learning results.
Stage 2: Determine acceptable evidence of learning.
Stage 3: Plan learning experiences and instruction.

It is "backward" because the process of design (outcome-assessment-activity) is in reverse order of its implementation. The main advantages of backward design are for us to stay focused on learning objectives when we design learning experience and to connect assessment directly to learning. Such design takes practice to master. If you are not familiar with backward design, there are abundant resources available. For instance, the National Capital Language Resource Center at the George Washington University offers an online manual: *Teaching World Languages: A Practical Guide* (Cockey, Johnson, &

Table 2.1 How language classrooms looked in the past compared to today

In the past	Today
Students learned about the language (grammar)	Students learn to use the language
Teacher-centered class	Learner-centered with teacher as facilitator/collaborator
Focused on isolated skills (listening, speaking, reading, and writing)	Focus on the three modes: interpersonal, interpretive, and presentational
Coverage of a textbook	Backward design focusing on the end goal
Using the textbook as the curriculum	Use of thematic units and authentic resources
Emphasis on teacher as presenter/lecturer	Emphasis on the relationship among the perspectives, practices, and produces of the culture
Use of technology as a "cool tool"	Integrating technology into instruction to enhance learning
Only teaching language	Using language as the vehicle to teach academic content
Same instruction for all students	Differentiating instruction to meet individual needs
Synthetic situations from textbook	Personalized real-world tasks
Confining language learning to the classroom	Seeking opportunities for learners to use language beyond the classroom
Testing to find out what students don't know	Assessing to find out what students can do
Only the teacher knows criteria for grading	Students know and understand criteria on how they will be assessed by reviewing the task rubric
Students "turn in" work only for the teacher	Learners create to "share and publish" to audiences more than just the teacher

Keatley, 2014) for free, which includes detailed instruction and examples of backward design and has a Chinese edition available.

While backward design helps us to have an effective *process* for curriculum design, the foreign language standards help us to make sure the *content* we design is productive for improving learners' proficiency. To be used in conjunction with the Proficiency Guidelines, ACTFL published the original version of *Standards for Foreign Language Learning in the 21st Century* (National Standards in Foreign Language Education Project, 1999) and coined five standard areas that have been commonly referred to as the 5 Cs: Communication, cultures, connections, comparisons, and communities. The current edition: *World-Readiness Standards for Learning Languages* (ACTFL, 2014) has maintained the 5 Cs and provides clarification and elaboration on 11 standards listed under the 5 Cs to promote foreign language learning.

Unlike the ACTFL Proficiency Guidelines and Standards, CEFR does not have a list of standards to accompany the proficiency framework and guide instructional practice. However, it does offer a model of language use and learning that illustrates how multiple factors contribute to communication and should lead to a task-oriented approach in language instruction:

> Language use, embracing language learning, comprises the actions performed by persons who as individuals and as social agents develop a range of **competences**, both **general** and in particular **communicative language competences**. They draw on the competences at their disposal in various contexts under various **conditions** and under various **constraints** to engage in **language activities** involving **language processes** to produce and/or receive **texts** in relation to **themes** in specific **domains**, activating those **strategies** which seem most appropriate for carrying out the **tasks** to be accomplished. The monitoring of these actions by the participants leads to the reinforcement or modification of their competences.
>
> (Council of Europe, 2009, p. 9, emphases in original)

This task-oriented model of language use is represented in Figure 2.1, which shows that language activities are interactions between the user's cognitive competences (strategies, processes, and knowledge) and the social context (domain of use):

Using these standards and models to guide the adoption of technology helps language teachers stay focused on the activities that promote communication and scaffold the development of linguistic and cultural competences. It also helps teachers avoid falling into the trap Wiggins and McTighe (2005) called a major "sin" of design: *hands-on without being minds-on* (p. 16), where the class activity appears engaging but leads to little meaningful learning. It is especially important when we evaluate technologies, because otherwise it is very easy to get lost in the fun and engaging activities made possible

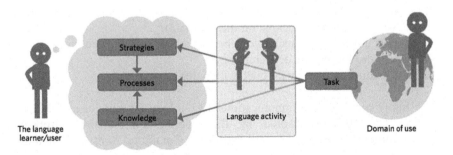

Figure 2.1 A representation of the CEFR's model of language use and learning
Reprinted from *Using the CEFR: Principles of good practice* (University of Cambridge, ESOL Examinations, 2011, p. 7)

by technology. For instance, I once observed a middle school Chinese class in which the teacher assigned her students the task of playing vocabulary games on the computer: shooting the meteors that carry the right words on the screen based on the given definition and flipping cards to match images with corresponding words. This activity lasted for about 15 minutes, which is one-third of her class time. While students were all *engaged* and excited about the games, the actual learning was very limited: memorization of vocabulary. If the teacher had designed her lesson from the standards/principles of language use and learning, she would have realized that such activity provided little opportunity for learners to actually communicate in the target language, make a connection to real-world language practice, or gain valuable linguistic/cultural insight. She would have designed her lesson very differently and used the precious contact hours more effectively.

Filter 3: The tool

The third and final filter to use when assessing and selecting technology is the properties of the actual tool and how well they fit with the designed learning experience. Many organizations have provided guidelines or checklists to help teachers choose. For instance, the International Society for Technology in Education has just released a new version of their Standards for Educators in 2017,[1] which detailed seven roles educators play in the practice of technology-enhanced instruction, namely the learner, the leader, the citizen, the collaborator, the designer, the facilitator, and the analyst. Detailed descriptions of objectives for each role may be found on their website: www.iste.org/standards/for-educators.

The Curriculum Leadership Institute proposed five points of consideration to help teachers reflect on their use of instructional technology (http://cliweb.org/five-points-for-evaluating-use-of-technology-in-the-classroom/):

1. Analyze and describe exactly what equipment you have available and when it is available.
2. Consider and rank the reasons to integrate technology into the classroom (a list of reasons is provided on their website).
3. Decide how available technology best enhances your curriculum.
4. Model productive use of technology.
5. Use technology to stay in touch with parents.

The Information and Communications Technology for Language Teachers Project (ICT4LT), sponsored by the Commission of the European Communities and European Association for Computer Assisted Language Learning (EUROCALL), provides a checklist and evaluation form for software and websites at www.ict4lt.org/en/index.htm.

Many national or state departments of education, schools, and universities may also have their own standards and/or guidelines for instructional

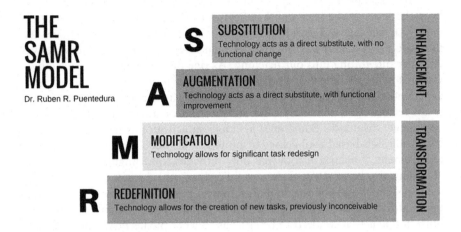

Figure 2.2 The SAMR model

This figure was created by Steve Garvie and was downloaded from Wikimedia commons at https://commons.wikimedia.org/wiki/File:The_SAMR_Model.jpg. License link: https://creativecommons.org/licenses/by-sa/4.0/deed.en

technology that teachers may refer to when they need to make decisions regarding incorporating technology in their educational practice.

One model that has been adopted by many teachers to evaluate technology is the SAMR model, which was popularized by Dr. Ruben R. Puentedura. As demonstrated in Figure 2.2, the SAMR model classified technologies into those that bring *substitution, augmentation, modification,* and *redefinition* to learning experiences, respectively.

In addition to being simple, straightforward, and easy to use, another important advantage of the SAMR model is that it does not only evaluate the technology in question, it evaluates how we use that technology to design learning experiences. A widespread YouTube video named "SAMR in 120 Seconds[2]" by Candace M used Google Docs as an example to demonstrate how you may use SAMR as a lens to evaluate the benefits a new technology brings to your classes: if you use Google Docs just as a text processer, then it is simply a *substitution* for other word-processing tools with no particular gains or functional changes; if you use it for accessing your document anywhere or sharing it with others, then it is *augmentation*, which has added or improved functions while the main task itself (i.e., word processing) remains unchanged; if Google Docs is used for learners to collaborate on one project, now this technology allows for significant task redesign and thus provides *modification* to the learning experience; finally, if you use Google Docs to connect and work with others across the world, a task that was previously inconceivable without incorporating this new technology, that enables a *redefinition* of the learning experience.

Using this model, we may weigh the benefits against the cost, including both the price of the tool and the effort put into learning and implementing it in your classes, and decide whether it is a preferable path to pursue. We may also use it to help us prioritize between several potential technologies we consider integrating into our teaching. As one may imagine, those technologies that bring modification and redefinition transform teaching and learning experiences and enable us to do more with our learners. However, it does not mean technologies that only offer substitution or augmentation should be completely dismissed. Sometimes a simple substitution is necessary, such as when one web-based tool ceases to provide a service and we need to find a replacement. Similarly, a tool that only provides some augmented functionality may also be worth consideration. For instance, if a new course management system allows you to communicate with parents more conveniently, you might still consider switching if that added function is valuable to you. The bottom line is that we need to be clear as to what the new technology brings us and whether it justifies the cost of its implementation.

In the next chapters many technologies will be mentioned that serve a wide range of purposes and it is simply impossible for anyone to integrate them all at the same time. I hope my readers will apply the filters mentioned in this chapter and evaluate and prioritize those technologies based on the knowledge of their learners, their instructional design, and a clear vision of the benefits each technology may bring to their classrooms.

Notes

1 The first version of the ISTE Standards for Teachers (renamed "Standards for Educators" in the latest 2017 version) was publicized in 2000 and then updated in 2008.
2 As of October, 8, 2017, this video at https://youtu.be/usOw823KY0g has accumulated 209,760 views.

References

ACTFL (2012). *ACTFL Proficiency Guidelines 2012*. Retrieved from www.actfl.org/publications/guidelines-and-manuals/actfl-proficiency-guidelines-2012
ACTFL (2014). *World-Readiness Standards for Learning Languages*. Retrieved from www.actfl.org/publications/all/world-readiness-standards-learning-languages
Council of Europe (2009). *Common European Framework of Reference for Languages: Learning, teaching, assessment*. Retrieved from https://rm.coe.int/1680459f97
Council of Europe (2017). *CEFR companion volume (Provisional edition)*. Retrieved from https://rm.coe.int/common-european-framework-of-reference-for-languages-learning-teaching/168074a4e2
Curtain, H. A., & Dahlberg, C. A. (2010). *Languages and children, making the match: New languages for young learners, grade K-8* (4th ed.). Boston, MA: Allyn & Bacon.
Cockey, S. W., Johnson, D., & Keatley, C. W. (2014). *Teaching world languages: A practical guide* (2nd ed.). Washington, DC: National Capital Language Resource Center. Retrieved from www.nclrc.org/TeachingWorldLanguages/index.html

Downes, T. (2002). Blending play, practice and performance: Children's use of the computer at home. *Journal of Educational Enquiry, 3*(2), 21–34.

Kennedy, G. E., Judd, T. S., Churchward, A., Gray, K., & Krause, K. L. (2008). First year students' experiences with technology: Are they really digital natives? *Australasian Journal of Educational Technology, 24*(1), 108–122.

Koivusilta, L. K., Lintonen, T. P., & Rimpelä, A. H. (2007). Orientations in adolescent use of information and communication technology: A digital divide by sociodemographic background, educational career, and health. *Scandinavian Journal of Public Health, 35*(1), 95–103.

Kvavik, R. B., Caruso, J. B., & Morgan, G. (2004). *ECAR study of students and information technology 2004: Convenience, connection, and control.* Boulder, CO: EDUCAUSE Center for Applied Research.

Lee, L. (2005). Young people and the Internet: From theory to practice. *Nordic Journal of Youth Research, 13*(4), 315–326.

Lenhart, A., Purcell, K., Smith, A., & Zickuhr, K. (2010). Social media & mobile Internet use among teens and young adults. Millennials. *Pew Internet & American Life Project*. Washington, DC: Pew Research Center.

National Association for the Education of Young Children & Fred Rogers Center (2012). *Selected examples of effective classroom practice involving technology tools and interactive media.* Retrieved from www.naeyc.org/files/naeyc/PS_technology_ Examples.pdf

National Standards in Foreign Language Education Project (1999). *Standards for Foreign Language Learning in the 21st Century* (SFFLL). Lawrence, KS: Allen Press.

Oliver, B., & Goerke, V. (2007). Australian undergraduates' use and ownership of emerging technologies: Implications and opportunities for creating engaging learning experiences for the Net generation. *Australasian Journal of Educational Technology, 23*(2), 171–186.

Partnership for 21st Century Learning (2011). *21st century skills map: World languages.* Retrieved from www.p21.org/storage/documents/Skills%20Map/p21_ worldlanguagesmap.pdf

Prensky, M. (2001). Digital natives, digital immigrants. *On the Horizon, 9*(5), 1–6.

Richards, J. C. (2013). Curriculum approaches in language teaching: Forward, central, and backward design. *Relc Journal, 44*(1), 5–33.

University of Cambridge, ESOL Examinations (2011). *Using the CEFR: Principles of good practice.* Cambridge, UK: Cambridge ESOL.

U.S. Department of Education (2010). Transforming American education: Learning powered by technology. *2016 National Education Technology Plan.* Washington, DC: U.S. Department of Education, Office of Educational Technology.

U.S. Department of Education (2016). Future ready learning: Reimagining the role of technology in education. *2016 National Education Technology Plan.* Washington, DC: U.S. Department of Education, Office of Educational Technology.

Wiggins, G. P., & McTighe, J. (2005). *Understanding by design.* Alexandria, VA: Association for Supervision and Curriculum Development.

3 Language learning process and points of enhancement using technology

What actually occurs in the learner's mind while learning a (foreign) language has been intriguing to psycholinguists, applied linguists, and language teachers for decades. Although scholars differ considerably in its pedagogical implication, it is agreed that language acquisition occurs via interaction between language input from the environment and the internal processing of the learner, which is represented in Figure 3.1.

What insight could language teachers draw from this process? First of all, in a foreign language learning context, *input* is often moderated by the teacher. The language input we choose for our learners should solidify learners' current proficiency while presenting new but comprehensible knowledge for learners to process. Although we may not control the learner's *internal processing*, we may instead carefully design the context of learning to help orient the learner's attention to the targeted learning points. To ensure learning, we could assess the learner's *output* against the preferred learning outcome. After assessment, we may provide feedback or further input to be processed, until learners successfully perform the preferred outcome. As you may see, from the perspective of pedagogical design, the learning process is not linear but rather cyclical, as represented in Figure 3.2.

In this chapter, we are going to discuss how technology can help enhance learning at each stage of this process.

Input: Abundant, authentic and comprehensible input

In a language class, learners may receive input from the text (including both written and spoken materials), the teacher, and their peer learners. The former two are highly moderated by the teacher with the learning objectives

Figure 3.1 Model of language acquisition (input processing)

Figure 3.2 Cyclical model of language acquisition from the perspective of pedagogical design

in mind while the last type is generated naturally by learners themselves when performing communication tasks. In this section, I will limit our discussion to the former two input types, because the input from peers is in fact the language *output* they generate. The design of tasks to solicit such output will be discussed later in this chapter.

In terms of teacher-moderated input, Krashen's theory of *Comprehensible Input* (1982, 1985) has largely impacted the field of foreign language education in the past decades and guided many language teachers to select appropriate input for their learners. The basic concept of comprehensible input can be formulated as $i+1$, with the italic i representing the learner's current proficiency level or possessed knowledge and 1 representing the immediate next step above it. For instance, learners who have learned to introduce their own names with "我叫……"("My name is…") may be ready to process the input about introducing others' names with "他／她叫……" ("His/her name is…").

By immersing learners in an environment where abundant input is provided at $i+1$ level, the input is comprehensible and the acquisition of the new knowledge (+1) will occur most naturally. To help teachers find the appropriate $i+1$ level for their learners, an indicator of this level is that learners are not yet able to produce the language but can already understand it in context.

When selecting text for comprehensible input, teachers should make sure the text is both abundant (quantity) and authentic (quality), and this is where technology may render its service. As mentioned in Chapter 1, one major advantage of using technology in language instruction is that technology, especially the Internet, grants learners access to authentic target language materials. For instance, video streaming services, including global ones (e.g., YouTube and Vimeo) and Chinese-specific ones, (e.g., 优酷/優酷, 腾讯视频/騰訊視頻, 哔哩哔哩/嗶哩嗶哩, and 爱奇艺/愛奇藝 [Youku, Tencent Video, Bilibili, and iQiyi]), provide myriad audiovisual sources of authentic input, such as movies, TV shows, commercials, news, pop songs, self-made videos, and screencasts. Nowadays, live webcasts (网络直播/網路直播) have been increasingly popular among Chinese celebrities or "web celebrities" (网红/網紅) and could provide rich data for linguistic and cultural discussion. Some popular platforms for such live webcasts include YY.com, 抖音 (Douyin.com) 火山小视频/火山小視頻 (Huoshan.com), and 美拍 Meipai.com. Many also use the live broadcast functions of social media such as Facebook, Instagram,

WeChat (微信), and Weibo (微博). When using such media, one important thing to keep in mind is content appropriateness, especially for younger learners. While there are many informative and culturally rich webcasts, some of them use extreme methods (e.g., revealing clothes; dangerous pranks) to attract an audience.

Similar to audiovisual materials, finding reading materials for learners of different levels has also been made easier thanks to the Internet. It is worth noting that such reading materials are not limited to texts in the form of articles, but may also include posts and comments, comic strips, memes, posters, email correspondence, instant messaging, etc. Even for novice learners whose text-types are limited to isolated words and formulaic sentences, there are ample selections of reading materials such as street names, bus schedules, banners, maps, store hours, or menus for them to decipher meanings and connect them to the written form of the language. Such materials may easily be found via a key word search of images on search engines such as Google, Yahoo, or 百度 (baidu.com). In 2016, a group of Chinese teachers also compiled a collection of such materials and published a free downloadable PDF: 真实语料学中文/ 真實語料學中文 *Authentic Materials for Chinese Teaching and Learning* (Liu, 2016. Downloadable at: www.teach-chinese.com/download/).

While it is a blessing for Chinese teachers to have access to such an abundance of Internet-accessible materials nowadays, the first challenge we are faced with is how to filter and select appropriate texts from the indefinite amount of raw materials. Keeping the principle of $i+1$ in mind may help us choose materials that align with what our learners are ready to learn.

It is also worth mentioning that the $i+1$ principle does not only apply to learners' *language* proficiency. In addition to the required proficiency level, knowledge of the certain *domain* of the text may also impact the learners' comprehension. Let's look at the CEFR's model of language use and learning once again:

As shown in this model, a task, which involves the use of text, does not happen in a vacuum. Instead, it occurs in a domain of use, which is defined

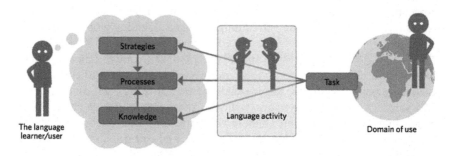

Reprint of Figure 2.1 A representation of the CEFR's model of language use and learning (University of Cambridge, ESOL Examinations, 2011, p. 7)

as "the broad sectors of social life in which social agents operate" (Council of Europe, 2009, p. 10). Lack of knowledge related to the domain would likely impede the learner's processing of the language activity. For instance, even a learner with advanced proficiency might not be ready to comprehend a broadcast about new evidence of gravitational waves despite the fact that the language used in the article fits well with their proficiency level. Domain-specific knowledge here is broadly defined and includes cultural awareness. For instance, the comprehension of a conversation in a business context may require knowledge about appropriate etiquette of formal meetings and expectations between business partners. When choosing such texts, teachers should first check learners' domain-specific knowledge and provide scaffolding accordingly, such as offering a glossary list, or explaining related cultural concepts.

Selection of texts is only the first step of input provision for our learners. To ensure comprehension and maximize learners' intake of the targeted knowledge, teachers need to design *tasks* to check learners' comprehension and promote meaningful communication on the basis of the text. We will discuss more about such interaction between texts and tasks and how technology may facilitate it in the next two chapters, focusing on developing learners' oral proficiency and literacy, respectively.

In addition to the text, another important source of input is the teacher's language use, which is partially why staying in the target language is highly encouraged if not mandated for language teachers. ACTFL, for instance, recommends that teachers remain in the target language as exclusively as possible (90% plus) at all levels of instruction (ACTFL, 2010). Use of technology may make it easier for the instruction to stay in the target language. As a teacher observed, "we've all found that there is very little that needs to be provided in English if you're using visuals and technology" (Crouse, 2012). By using presentational technology (e.g., PowerPoint, Keynote, Prezi, or Google Present), teachers are able to explain concepts, set up scenarios, and make their instruction much more comprehensible via the use of projected images and embedded multimedia.

One teaching method that relies heavily on teachers as the main source of input is Teaching Proficiency through Reading and Storytelling (TPRS).[1] As suggested in the name, the teacher's input takes a very specific and systemic form, that is, storytelling through three stages: 1) the teacher's storytelling (modeling), 2) story "asking" (telling the story jointly with learners' input), and 3) students' reading stories independently that contain the same structures used in the stages of storytelling and asking. The strengths of TPRS lie in it providing ample *repeated* input, which is a key to retention of learned vocabulary in long-term memory (Ray & Seely, 1998), and its storytelling activities engage and motivate learners (Braunstein, 2006; Blanton, 2015). What TPRS is not particularly equipped for is real-life situated tasks and use of authentic input[2] (Alley & Overfield, 2008; Blanton, 2015), compared to communicative language teaching (CLT). While it is not the purpose of this book to compare different teaching methods, I would like to remind my fellow language teachers to keep an open mind and see different methods as complementary to one another, rather than mutually exclusive. Movie Talk, a technique I am about to introduce in the next paragraph, is a great example that makes use of media materials and merges the advantages of both TPRS and CLT.

Developed by Dr. Ashley Hastings,[3] Movie Talk uses authentic videos by first showing them to the students for general understanding of the cultural and contextual settings, despite the fact that the language content itself might be beyond the learners' proficiency level, and then showing it for the second time when the audio is muted and replaced by the teacher's description of the scene, using the target language that suits learners' *i*+1 level. An example of Movie Talk looks like this (Contributor: Diane Neubauer, Valor Christian High School. The original teaching demo is available at: https://youtu.be/h707dWqAGIc):

1. The teacher shows the first two minutes of the movie 人在囧途 (Lost on Journey). The students only have very limited understanding of the language in it.
2. With a few target structures written on the board with English translation (e.g., 更好, 老板, 开玩笑/開玩笑, 回家过年/回家過年 [Better, boss, to joke, go home for the New Year]), the teacher plays the scene the second time, muted, and provides language input with repeated target structure:

(Simplified Chinese)

T: 有三个人，他们是工人。他 (pointing at the boss on screen) 是他们的老板。他是不好的老板。他不喜欢他的工人。他跟他们说话的时候，他说很多不好听的话，因为他不喜欢他们。他说，"我是你们的老板，可是你们是不好的工人。怎么有那么不好的工人？我不知道。你们很笨，也很不好。"所以他说，"你给我这个东西很不好，不要！很多人不要买，所以你们都很笨。"他说，"你们今年更笨；去年很笨，今年更笨。"还有他说，"你的头发很长，这是什么意思呢？因为头发很长说你脑子里很笨。" 他说得很不好听，对不对？很不喜欢他。他 (pointing at the scolded worker) 说，"我不要工作了。"他 (pointing at the boss) 说，"那，今天，你才聪明了。"懂了吗？差不多是这样的意思。
S: 老师，我有一个问题。"笨"是什么？
T: 哦，"笨"，Stupid. (Continue with the scene) 好吧，所以他的名字叫李成功。他的nickname叫灰太狼 – gray wolf，很不好的动物。还有，他的工作是什么？他是一个CEO。
S: 啊，我有……
T: 有个问题吗？
S: 还有一个问题。为什么他有stuffed animals?
T: 哦，对，因为他是老板，他是一个老板。他的工作是卖东西 (pointing to the stuffed animal as the product)。

(Traditional Chinese)

T: 有三個人，他們是工人。他(pointing at the boss on screen)是他們的老闆
。他是不好的老闆。他不喜歡他的工人。他跟他們說話的時候，他說
很多不好聽的話，因為他不喜歡他們。他說，"我是你們的老闆，可是
你們是不好的工人。怎麼有那麼不好的工人？我不知道。你們很笨，
也很不好。" 所以他說，"你給我這個東西很不好，不要！很多人不要
買，所以你們都很笨。" 他說，"你們今年更笨；去年很笨，今年更笨
。" 還有他說，"你的頭髮很長，這是什麼意思呢？因為頭髮很長說你
腦子裡很笨。" 他說得很不好聽，對不對？很不喜歡他。他 (pointing
at the scolded worker) 說，"我不要工作了。"他(pointing at the boss)
說，"那，今天，你才聰明了。"懂了嗎？差不多是這樣的意思。

S: 老師，我有一個問題。"笨"是什麼？

T: 哦，"笨"，Stupid. (Continue with the scene) 好吧， 所以他的名字叫李
成功。他的nickname叫灰太狼–gray wolf，很不好的動物。還有，他的
工作是什 麼？他是一個CEO。

S: 啊，我有……

T: 有個問題嗎？

S: 還有一個問題。為什麼他有stuffed animals？

T: 哦，對，因為他是老闆，他是一個老闆。他的工作是賣東西 (pointing
to the stuffed animal as the product)。

(English translation)

T: There are three people, and they are the workers. He (pointing at the
boss on screen) is their boss. He is a bad boss. He does not like his
workers. When he talks to them, he says lots of harsh words, because he
does not like them. He said, "I am your boss, but you are bad workers.
How could there be such bad workers? I don't understand. You are
stupid, and bad." So he said, "The thing you gave me was bad. I don't
want it. Many people don't want to buy it, so you are all stupid." He
said, "You are even more stupid this year. Last year you were stupid,
but this year even more stupid." And he said, "You have long hair.
What does that mean? Long hair means you have a stupid brain." He
said really harsh words, right? We don't like him. He (pointing at the
scolded worker) said, "I'm quitting." He (pointing at the boss) said,
"then you're smart today." Understand? That's roughly what the scene
is about.

S: Teacher, I have a question, what is "ben" (Chinese)?

T: Oh, "ben." Stupid. (Continue with the scene) Ok, so his name is Li
Chenggong. His nickname is Hui Tailang (Chinese) – gray wolf, a bad
animal. And, what's his job? He is a CEO.

S: Ah, I have…

T: Have a question?

S: I have one more question. Why does he have stuffed animals?

T: Oh, yes, because he is the boss. He is a boss and his job is to sell things (pointing to the stuffed animal as the product).

3.   Move on to the next scene and repeat the procedure.

As shown in this example, Movie Talk not only makes the media material engaging and interactive, but also successfully produces comprehensible input for learners of lower proficiency level while using authentic cultural scenes. The negotiation of meaning between the teacher and the learners is also highly communicative. Movie Talk is one example of combining language input with meaningful tasks but it is not the only way to do so. More types of tasks will be discussed in the next two chapters.

Internal processing: Raise attention and create environments supporting processing

While scholars may differ in their views on what actually goes on in the learner's mind during the processing of input (e.g., whether it involves a linguistic-specific processor or simply uses a frequency-based mechanism the same way learners acquire other knowledge; whether the process is the same for the first and second languages; whether the learner has conscious control over what their mind chooses to process, etc.), the consensus among scholars is that not *all* input would be processed and acquired in the end. Instead, only certain selected input is *noticed*, enters the learner's mind to be processed (i.e., de-coding, forming and testing hypotheses, etc.), and after processing becomes the final *intake*, which is considered acquired knowledge and ready for language production (Corder, 1967; Chaudron, 1985; Smith, 1986; Schmidt, 1990; Gass, 1997).

Since the processing occurs in the learner's mind, there is little teachers may actively do once the processing begins. However, some actions may be taken while providing language input to increase the opportunity for certain parts of the input to be *noticed* and enter the processing facility, such as repeatedly using the same vocabulary or grammar to increase frequency, slowing down or being louder to raise attention to certain phrases, or using gestures for emphasis. For instance, some teachers try to bring learners' attention to tones by associating each tone with a specific gesture. When providing language input, they use the gestures to make learners notice the tone. Similarly, when tones are the focus, some teachers present the written text with color-coding to remind learners to pay attention to tones. Some online dictionaries such as *MDBG* and *Written Chinese* have adopted color-coding for its entries. There are also tools to help teachers generate color-coding texts without having to manually change the color of each single character, such as the color-code Chinese text converter developed by Purple Culture (www.purpleculture.net/color-code-chinese-by-tone/).

Color-coding is not the only way to point learners to certain linguistic features, and the tone is also not the only linguistic feature that can be emphasized in a text. When presenting a written text, teachers may use emphatic styling such as underlines, shading, or text effects (e.g., italic or bold fonts, shadows or glows, etc.) to help learners notice certain parts of the text. One thing to remember when using such styling though is not to overuse it. Use the effects consistently (e.g., always use underlines for grammar structures, or always use red text for targeted vocabulary, etc.) and try to keep it simple. Remember, if we mark too many things with emphasis, we are actually distracting the learner's focus and it defeats the purpose of emphasizing. Similarly, although some fancy effects (e.g., flashing or bouncing characters) are exciting and do attract learner's attention, the attention itself may be paid primarily to the cool effect itself rather than the targeted learning point.

In addition to using these methods to direct learners' attention to specific parts of input, teachers may also attempt to lower learners' *affective filters*, the negative emotional responses to the learning environment (e.g., performance anxiety, peer pressure, or fear of being corrected/punished/ridiculed). Since affective filters may impact cognitive functionality, it is important that we as teachers maintain an environment of high self-esteem, high self-confidence, and low anxiety to prevent "mental blocks" and facilitate acquisition. To create such an environment does not necessarily require utilizing technology, but as mentioned in Chapter 1, studies have shown that learners may find learning in an e-environment less stressful and threatening, and thus a valid alternative to traditional classroom settings. For face-to-face classrooms, on the other hand, game-based learning is one way to help learners associate learning with positive emotions, which many technological tools could be of help with; this will be discussed in Chapter 7.

Another effective yet often neglected way to lower learners' affective filter is to simply give them enough time to complete their processing. That is, allow learners a *silence period*, in Krashen's words (1982). Tolerance of silence is one important ability I always try to remind new teachers in the field to hone. Most if not all teachers are naturally eager to help our learners and sometimes it misleads us to regard learners' silence as a lack of or struggle with comprehension and to jump in prematurely to supply more input, including that provided in the form of well-intended hints or words of encouragement. In many cases, what the learner needs is just time for them to complete the processing. At this point, attempting to intervene is at best unnecessary, and at worst distracting. In day-to-day classroom practice, even a wait of ten more seconds (believe me, it feels longer than that and you just have to power through it) before we jump in to "help" makes a huge difference.

Output: Pushed comprehensible output

While scholars tend to agree that ample comprehensible input is necessary for second language acquisition, their views of the roles output and feedback play in second language acquisition diverge considerably. According to Krashen's input hypothesis, ample comprehensible input is both *necessary* and *sufficient* for acquisition, and production of language will follow naturally once the input is successfully processed internally. However, some studies have shown that comprehensible input alone might not necessarily lead to proficiency when it comes to language production, even after years of exposure (Swain 1985; Harley, 1988; Bley-Vroman, 1989). *Comprehensible output*, which encourages learners to speak and write in their second language and negotiate meaning through interaction, also plays a significant role in acquisition. Swain and colleagues (Swain & Lapkin, 1995; Swain, 2005) have identified five basic functions of comprehensible output:

- When learners attempt production, they may notice a gap of linguistic knowledge that they may be able to comprehend but not yet produce. The notice of such a gap triggers further processing and thus may lead to cognitive generation of new knowledge, or consolidation of previously possessed knowledge.
- Output functions as the main venue where learners test the hypotheses of the target language formed during processing. Through interaction with others, learners receive important feedback as to whether their language use successfully conveys the intended meaning, which may lead to confirmation or adjustment of their hypotheses formed during internal processing.
- When negotiating and resolving linguistic problems, learners develop *metalanguage*, which is the language used to talk *about* language. Being able to think, describe, and discuss their linguistic choices helps develop learners' association between form and meaning. When learners put their working hypotheses in language, it also makes their knowledge and learning strategies more observable and easier for the teacher to provide relevant and effective feedback.
- Production of output promotes automatization of language use. In particular, *fluency* is something that may not be developed without ample opportunity to actually speak the language. Learners may also gain self-confidence with frequent successful target language production.
- Output enables learners to move from a semantic to a syntactic use of language. When processing input, learners focus on comprehending the meaning (semantic knowledge). Only when they are asked to produce language do they need to organize their ideas into sentences and longer text, which leads them to pay attention to the syntactic standards of the target language, such as sentence structure, parts of speech, and word order, etc.

In order to harness these functions that benefit learning, *forcing* learners to produce language, namely by designing tasks that require production and interaction, is deemed necessary (Swain, 1985). There are many types of tasks that may push learners to produce language output. For instance, "information gap" is one such task that many teachers include in their lesson designs to have learners engage in meaningful communication. An information gap task gives each learner partial information and they must communicate with one another to fill in the gaps in order to complete the task (Ellis, 2003). For instance, two students may each have a personal schedule for the next week (assigned or made by the students themselves), and their goal is to find some time to meet up. In order to achieve this goal, they will have to use the target language to ask and answer about their availability, give reasons, agree and disagree, and finally reach a solution that works for them. Such activities guarantee the production of the target language and negotiation in the process, and tend to be highly relevant to the theme of the current lesson unit. In addition to information gap, other commonly used task types for output production include: presentation (on personal or public topics: individual or collaborative), discussion, debate, and situated role play, and writing tasks for different purposes and in different genres.

How does technology assist in these tasks and enhance comprehensible output? Technology can help with the production of comprehensible output in the following ways:

- It helps to simulate real-life situations to contextualize the task. Such contextualization may involve the use of images, music/sound, videos, and props. For instance, in a "giving directions" task, learners may use Beijing Zoo's online map (displayed on a projected screen, on learners' mobile devices, or as printouts) to give directions and help others find the panda house. Google Maps is also a good tool for direction-related tasks. If we aim to encourage learners to perform the function of apology, we may have them watch a clip where one character offends another, and ask learners to do a role play that follows the scene, or assume the role of the offending character and write an email to apologize. Use of technology helps make the task more realistic and engaging.
- Technology provides alternative venues where comprehensible output may occur. This function is especially powerful when we consider the factor of time/exposure. Imagine we have our intermediate-level learners tell a story about a forgetful friend. In the setting of prepared speech, the presentation of the story may last 3–5 minutes for each student. That means, in an average language class that has 15 students (in many schools there are more), the total class time spent on the presentation would be 45–75 minutes in a traditional classroom setting. While such in-class presentation offers valuable practice for learners to develop the skills and confidence for public speech, we might only be able to accommodate such tasks once or twice per semester due to limited class hours. To increase learners' opportunity for such practice, we may instead have students record their speech in the form of audio, videos, or narrated slideshow. Tools and techniques for such tasks will be introduced in the next chapter in the section on technologies for oral communication tasks.
- Technology expands the scope of output tasks. For instance, learners may send one another text messages, write and respond to posts on social

media, email a pen pal (or often called a "key pal") in a sister program in China, make a comic strip or animated cartoon online, or have a live conference interviewing a native speaker. Some of these tasks may be done without the assistance of technology, such as interviewing a native speaker face to face, or writing a physical letter to a Chinese pen pal, but admittedly, technology has made such tasks easier to arrange and execute.

- Technology may help learners feel more comfortable using the language. As mentioned earlier, the e-environment is regarded as less threatening by many learners and thus they may be more willing to speak or write more in such communication venues. Many learners also enjoy creating avatar or cartoon characters to carry out a dialogue, or dubbing for a movie scene (more information about tools and techniques for such tasks can be found in the next chapter). Appealing to the fun factor of language learning in such activities may also contribute to lowering learners' affective filters and facilitate learning.

Feedback: Consistent, focused, intense, and individualized feedback

Except for those who subscribe to nativist theory[4] (e.g., Krashen, 1981, 1982; Schwartz, 1993; Truscott, 1999), most SLA scholars support the notion that teachers' corrective feedback plays an important role in language acquisition (e.g., Carroll, Roberge, & Swain, 1992; Carroll & Swain, 1993; Long, Inagaki, & Ortega, 1998; Ellis, 2006; Ellis, Basturkmen, & Loewen, 2001; Oliver, 1995, 2000; Spada & Lightbown, 1993; Russell, 2009). In practice, provision of corrective feedback is also commonly observed in classrooms. I have personally yet to meet one teacher who claims that they do not provide corrective feedback at all to their students. However, less converging and sometimes directly oppositional views may be found both among scholars and among teachers as to the effectiveness of different types of feedback. This section will introduce these different types briefly and discuss how technology may assist their provision but will not engage in the debate about their effectiveness since certain types of feedback may benefit certain types of learners more than others (e.g., adults vs. younger learners; higher vs. lower proficiency levels; learners with different individual learning styles, etc.). It ultimately depends on the teacher in practice to observe their learners closely and choose the types of feedback that work the best for them.

Corrective feedback may be broadly divided into two categories: implicit and explicit correction, depending on whether the teacher tries to *overtly* point out the error they made and provide the corrected form. Lyster and colleagues (Lyster & Ranta, 1997; Panova & Lyster, 2002; Lyster & Mori, 2006) have identified several types of feedback in each category and I will provide examples of each type using a learner's utterance with a common error: 我刚才看了一只狗/我剛才看了一隻狗。 (I just "watched" a dog, instead of "saw" a dog.)

Implicit feedback types

Repetition: 你刚才"看"了一只狗？(You just "watched" a dog?)

In this type of feedback, the teacher simply repeats the learner's erroneous utterance but with paralinguistic clues such as change of intonation, pauses, facial expressions, or gestures to indicate some changes need to be made to reformulate the utterance.

Recast: 你刚才"看见"了一只狗。/ 你剛才"看見"了一隻狗。(You just "saw" a dog.) Or a two-stage recast in combination with repetition: 你刚才"看"了一只狗？ 你刚才"看见"了一只狗。/ 你剛才"看"了一隻狗？你剛才"看見"了一隻狗。(You just "watched" a dog? You just "saw" a dog.)

Defined as "teacher's reformulation of all or part of a student's utterance, minus the error" (Lyster & Ranta, 1997, p. 46), recast is done with the teacher providing the correct form, often accompanied by paralinguistic clues to direct the learner's attention to the corrected part.

Clarification request: 你说什么？/ 你說什麼？(What did you say?) This type of feedback takes the form of common clarification questions, and gives learners the opportunity to correct or clarify themselves without directly pointing out the type or location of the error.

Elicitation:

Form 1: 这句话应该怎么说？/ 這句話應該怎麼說？(How should we say this sentence?) This form directly asks learners to reformulate the utterance.

Form 2: 你刚才"什么"了一只狗？/ 你剛才"什麼"了一隻狗？ (You just "what" a dog?) This form uses a question word in place of the error.

Form 3: 你刚才......？/ 你剛才......？ (You just...?) This form uses a strategic pause to invite learners to complete the utterance with a corrected form.

Elicitation also gives learners the opportunity for self-correction. The difference between clarification request and elicitation is that the latter makes learners aware of the existence/location of errors in their original utterance.

Translation: You just "watched" a dog?

Technically, translation may take the form of any of the types mentioned above. The difference is just the feedback is done in learners' native language (L1) instead of the target language (L2).

Explicit feedback types

Explicit correction: 我们不说"看"了一只狗，应该说"看见"了一只狗。/ 我們不說"看"了一隻狗，應該說"看見"了一隻狗。(We don't say "watched" a dog. We should say "saw" a dog.)

Explicit correction overtly contrasts erroneous with corrected utterances.

Metalinguistic feedback: Although in Chinese both 看 and 看见/看見 involve the use of one's vision, 看 refers to the intentional performance of the action such as 看电视/看電視 and 看书/看書 [Watch TV and read a book], while 看见/看見 emphasizes the spontaneous result of the action, the reception of the visual signal, when you actually "see" something.

Metalinguistic feedback provides information *about* the error and explain *why* the error is considered unacceptable in the target language. In lower-level classes, such feedback often involves the teacher's code-switching from the target language to learners' L1 because the required linguistic competence for processing such information is beyond the learners' current proficiency.

Table 3.1 compares the general pros and cons of explicit and implicit feedback.

In addition to the types of feedback, the manner in which a teacher gives feedback may also impact learners' uptake. The preferred feedback provision should reflect:

• Consistency, in terms of the format and the occurrence of feedback. For instance, Doughty (2001) observed a teacher who maintained consistency by always allowing learners to repair their own errors and giving the targeted reformulation only if the learners failed to do so. Using consistent paralinguistic cues may also help learners to notice when the

Table 3.1 Pros and cons of implicit and explicit feedback

	Pros	Cons
Implicit Feedback	• Learners are given the opportunity to correct themselves. • Learners may be pushed to produce more comprehensible output. • The flow of communication is less interrupted than explicit feedback.	• Given its indirect nature, there is more ambiguity in implicit feedback and learners may get confused or not notice the error. • Learners may not necessarily be able to infer the underlying rules pertaining to the error.
Explicit Feedback	• It draws learners' attention to the error and reformulation more directly. • The feedback is clearer and thus requires less "guessing" from the learners. • It gives more information about the existence, location, and nature of the error.	• It does not give room for learners to correct themselves. • It may cause learners to feel criticized and have negative affective impact on learners' confidence and motivation.[7] • It takes the learners further out of the task context and causes more interruption of the communication flow.

corrective feedback is happening and orient their attention to the contrastive reformulation (Chaudron, 1977; Lightbown & Spada, 1990). The occurrence of feedback should also be consistent (Han, 2002). When it is the same type of error, correcting some and leaving others uncorrected might cause confusion. However, it does not mean that we should correct *every* error the learners make, which brings us to the next principle: focus.

- Focus. The consistent correction should focus on certain systematic, *global* errors (Hendrickson, 1978) instead of trying to correct *all* errors. When a teacher targets too wide a range of errors, it may overwhelm learners, impede the development of fluency, and have a negative impact on learners' self-confidence and motivation (Ellis, 2009; Storch, 2010).
- Intensity. Intensity involves the frequency of correction. The frequency of correction of a repeated error leads to saliency, and subsequent retention. Han (2002) pointed out that intensity and focus should work together in order to ensure reliable uptake. If a type of error does not occur frequently, it would not be considered a "global" focus and simply will not provide enough incidences for intense correction.
- Individualization. When giving feedback, teachers should keep in mind that what we assume to be salient might not be recognized as salient to learners (Smith, 1991). Close observation and adaption to individual learners' processing preference and readiness is thus crucial to feedback provision (Han, 2002; Sheen, 2006). It is also worth pointing out that although there are indeed common errors in (given groups of) learners' L2 output, there might also be consistent errors shown in individual learners' output, which is another reason for individualized feedback. Learners tend to enjoy the personalized nature of such feedback and consider it beneficial for their learning (Hsu, Wang, & Comac, 2008).

Technology may provide means and tools for teachers to offer consistent, focused, intense, and individualized feedback, in the following ways:

- Technology may help us to collect and store learners' output as audio files, videos, or digital text documents. It enables the teachers to review learners' language use asynchronously and conduct more systematic analysis to identify frequent errors and choose their corrective foci accordingly. Accumulated output over time may also allow teachers to observe learners' uptake of correction and further adjust their feedback to follow up. Take the following course video-blog for example (Contributor: Amber Navarre, Boston University). The learners were asked to respond once a week to an episode of 《蜗居》 (*Dwelling Narrowness*), a Chinese TV series, in the format of a recorded speech video posted on the course blog. In this example, the teacher noticed a mix of registers (formal and informal) in a learner's output, which is very common when learners are transitioning from intermediate to advanced proficiency and from a personal communicative domain to a public/professional domain. Therefore, in her feedback to the learner's week 2 assignment, the teacher suggested:

(Simplified Chinese)
你可能要统一一下你说话的风格，比如，你说"在吃饭时"，
这是比"(在)吃饭的时候"正式的说法，但是"我爸／我妈" 是非常口语
的说法，所以听起来就会一下子正式，一下子口语。下次可以试着统
一你说话的风格。

(Traditional Chinese)
你可能要統一一下你說話的風格，比如，你說"在吃飯時"，這是比"（
在）吃飯的時候"正式的說法，但是"我爸／我媽"是非常口語的說法，
所以聽起來就會一下子正式，一下子口語。下次可以試著統一你說話
的風格。

(English translation)
You probably want to unify the style of your speech. For instance, you
said "when we ate" (more formal Chinese). It was a more formal expres-
sion than "when we ate" (less formal Chinese), but "my pop/mom" is on
the other hand quite colloquial, so it sounds formal for one second and
colloquial for the next. Next time, you can try to unify the style when
you talk.

A few more corrections regarding the formal/informal registers occurred
in week 3–5, and the learner made adjustments occurring to the teacher's
suggestions. Noticing the learner's uptake, the teacher commented in her feedback to the learner's assignment in week 6:

> 你现在说话比之前正式了，比较少过于口语的表达方式，
> 这一点非常好。／你現在說話比以前正式了，比較少過-
> 於口語的表達方式，這一點非常好。(You now talk more formally than
> before, with less overly colloquial expressions. It is very good.)

Without the video-blog that stored learners' speech data, the teacher might
not have been able to identify learners' global error and trace their uptake
of earlier corrective feedback. The noticing and commenting on learners'
improvement also brings us to an important concept that teacher feedback
does not necessarily have to be strictly "corrective" but can also recognize and
reinforce the learners' positive changes in their output that indicate learning.
It is worth noting that studies have also cautioned teachers to be careful when
giving praise for reinforcement. While it does have a positive affective impact
on learners' motivation and confidence, it should be *proportionate* to the actual
language performance and accompanied by a clear indication as to why they
are praised. Excessive and vague praise may be interpreted by the learners as
indicating that the teacher has little confidence in them (Thompson, 1997).

- The availability of recorded output from learners also helps teachers to
  provide individualized feedback. The individualization may reify in two

ways: 1) by recognizing individual learners' language pattern and providing customized correction or reinforcement; 2) by incorporating a personalized tone to the feedback and showing genuine interest from the teacher in *what* the learner actually says (the content), not just *how* they say it (the form). For instance, the whole comment the teacher gave the aforementioned learner for his week 6 assignment reads:

(Simplified Chinese)
说 得 很 好 。 "幸 福 的 概 念 是 要 先 有 物 质 才 能 考 虑 的 " 的 这 个 想 法 表 达 得 很 好 。 （ 但 是 你 后 来 收 回 了 …… 哈哈，我想你的意思是，我们需要基本的物质，不然不可能幸福，但是其他超过这些基本物质的东西就不一定有必要了。）你现在说话比之前正式了，比较少过于口语的表达方式，这一点非常好。
语言建议：
　如果我没有好好律师的话 》》如果我没有好"的"律师的话
　我在这边的物质的价值会增加在那边 》》 （这句话我有一点不懂，你是说如果拿美国赚的钱去其他那些地方就能得到更多的物质享受，因为物价比较低，是这个意思吗？）

(Traditional Chinese)
說 得 很 好 。 "幸 福 的 概 念 是 要 先 有 物 質 才 能 考 慮 的 " 的 這 個 想 法 表 達 得 很 好 。 （ 但 是 你 后 來 收 回 了 …… 哈哈，我想你的意思是，我們需要基本的物質，不然不可能幸福，但是其他超過這些基本物質的東西就不一定有必要了。）你現在說話比之前正式了，比較少過於口語的表達方式，這一點非常好。
語言建議：
　如果我沒有好好律師的話 》》如果我沒有好"的"律師的話
　我在這邊的物質的價值會增加在那邊 》》 （這句話我有一點不懂，你是說如果拿美國賺的錢去其他那些地方就能得到更多的物質享受，因為物價比較低，是這個意思嗎？）

(English translation)
Well said. "The concept of spiritual happiness can only come into consideration after material fulfillment" was a well-expressed thought. (But you took it back later… haha. I think what you meant was that we need basic material, or otherwise we cannot really claim happiness, but it's not necessary to possess material beyond the basic needs.) You now talk more formally than before, with less overly colloquial expressions. It is very good.
Language suggestions:
If I don't have well lawyers 》》 If I don't have "good" lawyers, the value of my material here will increase there 》》 I am a little confused about this sentence. Do you mean if we take the money we make in the US to other places, we can then enjoy more material benefits, because the living standards are lower in the latter? Is that what you meant?

In this comment, the teacher provided her personal interpretation of the learner's talk (我想你的意思是……/ I think what you meant was...), expressed her amusement at seeing that the learner gave an argument and then second-guessed himself as the talk progressed (但是你后来收回了，哈哈 / 但是你後來收回了，哈哈 / you took it back later... haha) and her confusion about one specific sentence (这句话我有一点不懂，你是说…… / 這句話我有一點不懂，你是說……/ I am a little confused about this sentence. Do you mean...). The tone of these comments conveyed to the learner that what they said was important and was being treated with due attention. It is also worth pointing out that the manner of the teacher-provided feedback is consistent with all the video posts through the semester, with more content-oriented feedback first, followed by linguistic suggestions.

Although such individualized feedback can also be achieved in a traditional classroom setting, the frequency of its provision may be considerably increased with the utilization of technology. In this example, the learner's recorded speech was 6 minutes long. If it had occurred in a traditional classroom, the speech and the following feedback would have easily taken up multiple class periods for an average class of 15 students. It would not have been possible to conduct such activities with the same frequency, namely once a week in this case.

- Technology may make feedback less interruptive and favors intense and consistent feedback. Depending on the timing of provision, feedback can be immediate or delayed. Immediate feedback addresses the error when it occurs, while delayed feedback is given after the communication event is completed. Immediate feedback makes it easier for learners to match the correction with the targeted error. However, an unavoidable disadvantage is that it interrupts the communication flow, especially given that a certain wait-time needs to be allowed for learners to process the correction before they can go back to the communication task (James, 1998; Lyster, 1998). Delayed feedback, on the other hand, does not interrupt the communication flow, but may make it harder for learners to locate the errors, especially in a speaking task where learners may simply not remember exactly what they said even just minutes ago.

  Technology may help us to an extent to combine the advantages of immediate feedback (clear mapping of correction to error) and delayed feedback (uninterrupted communication flow). With recording technology, for instance, the feedback is given after the communication task is completed and is delayed by default. However, when receiving feedback, learners may replay the video/audio to help them remember their own speech. Some tools may further enable teachers to insert their feedback into the original video/audio, to the exact point where the error occurred. This method in a sense reconstructs the "immediacy" of the feedback and maps the correction directly to the targeted error. For instance,

VideoNot.es allows users to make notes while watching a YouTube video and "timestamp" it with your notes. It generates a sharable Google doc with the notes, and when clicking on each note, it brings you back to the relevant part of video.

VideoNot.es is currently limited to text feedback. If a teacher would prefer to add a video/audio comment, they may do so by using video/audio editing tools (e.g., GarageBand or Audacity for audio; iMovie, Shotcut, Filmora, or Camtasia for videos[5]) to record their feedback into learners' original files. Take GarageBand for example, as shown in Figure 3.3: the teacher may pause the learner's audio when they hear a targeted error, split the original track, record their own feedback in a separate track, and export one audio file at the end.

Another option that works with videos is to use online interactive content-embedding tools, such as Edpuzzle and PlayPosit, to record and embed your voices into a self-uploaded video, or a streamed video (e.g., YouTube or Vimeo). Figure 3.4 is an example of embedding a voice recording to a YouTube video in Edpuzzle by using its "record audio notes" function. If you have learners upload their videos on streaming services, Edpuzzle and PlayPosit would be quite convenient and easy tools for giving audio feedback.

- As demonstrated in the case of inserted feedback above, technology allows the teacher to provide feedback in both oral and written modes. While oral feedback may include the reformulated speech input (i.e., the teacher says the utterance correctly) for the learners to model, written feedback may benefit learning when it comes to metalinguistic explanations (Bitchener,

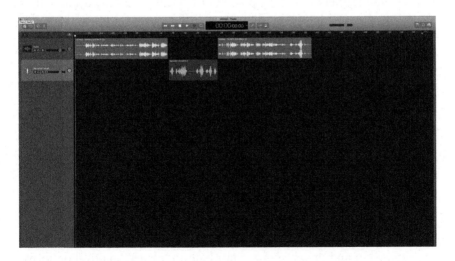

Figure 3.3 Example of recorded in-speech feedback using GarageBand

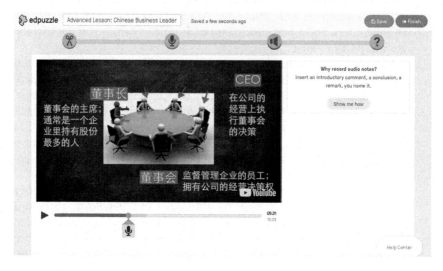

Figure 3.4 Example of recorded in-speech feedback using Edpuzzle

2008; Ellis, Sheen, Murakami, & Takashima, 2008). Most blogging and services (e.g., Weebly, Blogger, and Wordpress) and learning management systems (e.g., Blackboard, Moodle, Canvas, and Google Classroom) allow teachers to leave both written feedback as typed comments and video/ audio feedback either through file attachment or direct recording. In the next chapter, I will introduce several tools that are designed particularly to collect learners' speech output (e.g., FlipGrid, Voicethread, and Lingt), which also tend to provide an easy one-click comment recording option for teachers as well as typed comments.

It is worth pointing out that many of the tools mentioned above also allow peer commenting. Teachers may encourage learners to view each other's work and leave feedback. While peer feedback tends not to be corrective in nature and might not directly contribute to the development of oral proficiency, it does add value to two aspects of learning:

- It helps cultivate an interactive and collaborative learner community and develop learners' social identity in the target language (Conrad, 2005; Harrison & Thomas, 2009; Sung & Mayer, 2012).
- It gives learners' presentational work a wider audience[6] and makes the communication more meaningful and purposeful compared to just submitting the work to the teacher for correction/grading. This sense of authorship and presence may contribute to learners' motivation to use the target language more frequently (Richardson, 2006; Sun, 2009).

In this chapter, we have discussed how technology may help facilitate the learning process in different stages. The next chapter will focus on technologies that enhance learners' development of oral proficiency.

Resources

1. Streaming video services:
   YouTube: www.youtube.com
   Vimeo: vimeo.com
   优酷 / 優酷: www.youku.com
   腾讯视频 / 騰訊視頻: http://v.qq.com
   哔哩哔哩 / 嗶哩嗶哩: www.bilibili.com
   爱奇艺 / 愛奇藝: www.iqiyi.com
2. Live webcast services:
   YY: www.yy.com
   火山小视频: www.huoshanzhibo.com
   美拍: www.meipai.com/live
   Facebook: www.facebook.com
   Instagram: www.instagram.com
   微信: www.wechat.com/en/
   微博 / 微博: https://weibo.com
3. Search engines:
   Google: www.google.com
   Yahoo: www.yahoo.com
   百度: www.baidu.com

Tools

1. Tools for inserting comments in learners' speech videos/audio:

Product Name	VideoNot.es
Function	Insert timestamped text comments in YouTube videos
Difficulty Level	★☆
Product Website	www.videonot.es

Product Name	Camtasia
Function	Make video/audio comments to learners' video/audio
Difficulty Level	Basic recording: ★
	Advanced editing: ★★★
Product Website	www.techsmith.com/video-editor.html

Product Name	iMovie (Mac)
Function	Make video/audio comments to learners' video/audio
Difficulty Level	Basic recording: ★
	Advanced editing: ★★☆
Product Website	www.apple.com/imovie/

Product Name	Shotcut
Function	Edit videos
Difficulty Level	★☆
Product Website	www.shotcut.org

Product Name	Filmora
Function	Edit videos
Difficulty Level	★☆
Product Website	https://filmora.wondershare.net/filmora-video-editor.html

Product Name	Edpuzzle
Function	Make audio comments to learners' video
Difficulty Level	★☆
Product Website	https://edpuzzle.com/

Product Name	Playposit
Function	Embed interactive content into a video
Difficulty Level	★☆
Product Website	www.playposit.com

Product Name	GarageBand (Mac only)
Function	Make audio comments to learners' audio
Difficulty Level	Simple recording: ★ Advanced editing: ★★
Product Website	www.apple.com/mac/garageband/

Product Name	Audacity
Function	Make audio comments to learners' audio
Difficulty Level	Simple recording: ★ Advanced editing: ★★
Product Website	www.audacityteam.org

2. Blogging tools:

Product Name	Weebly
Function	Create and maintain blogs
Difficulty Level	★★
Product Website	www.weebly.com

Product Name	Blogger
Function	Create and maintain blogs
Difficulty Level	★★
Product Website	www.blogger.com

Product Name	Wordpress
Function	Create and maintain blogs
Difficulty Level	★★★
Product Website	https://wordpress.com

3.   Tools for collecting learners' speech output:

Product Name	Flipgrid
Function	Collect and organize learners' speech videos; teacher and peer feedback
Difficulty Level	★
Product Website	https://info.flipgrid.com

Product Name	Voicethread
Function	Collect learners' narration with images; teacher and peer feedback
Difficulty Level	★☆
Product Website	https://voicethread.com

Product Name	Lingt
Function	Collect individual learners' audio and text responses; teacher feedback
Difficulty Level	★
Product Website	www.lingt.com

Notes

1 The TPRS method draws heavily on the theory of comprehensible input, and many teachers practicing it actually call the method "Comprehensible Input." However, since TPRS is not the only teaching method that applies the principle of comprehensible input, this book differentiates its use of TPRS (a teaching method) and comprehensible input (a language processing theory) to avoid confusion.
2 A common definition of "authentic" language use is that it is intended for native speakers with a real-life goal. In TPRS, the "stories" are created for the purpose of language learning and thus not intended for native speakers; they are not considered "authentic" language input.
3 An overview and examples of movie talk may be found on her website: http://glesismore.com/movietalk/preview.html
4 Nativist theory was coined by Chomsky, who argued for the innateness of language acquisition. This view has impacted Krashen's input theory that comprehension input is sufficient for internal processing and instruction/feedback is not only unnecessary but could even be distractive and harmful to learners' processing.
5 All of these video editing tools may also be used to edit audio-only files.
6 The audience may involve the general public in an open blog and social media setting, or be limited to the class and authorized users in a password-protected blog or private social media setting (e.g., a closed Facebook group page or an Edmodo site).
7 Negative affective impact might be provoked by either implicit and explicit feedback, but is more common with the latter because the "correction" is made more obvious.

References

American Council on the Teaching of Foreign Languages (ACTFL) (2010). *Use of the target language in the classroom*. Retrieved from www.actfl.org

Alley, D., & Overfield, D. (2008). An analysis of the Teaching Proficiency through Reading and Storytelling (TPRS) method. *Dimension 2008*, 13–25.

Bitchener, J. (2008). Evidence in support of written corrective feedback. *Journal of Second Language Writing, 17*(2), 102–118.

Blanton, M. (2015). *The effect of two foreign language teaching approaches, communicative language teaching and teaching proficiency through reading and storytelling, on motivation and proficiency for Spanish III students in high school* (Doctoral dissertation, Liberty University).

Bley-Vroman, R. (1989). What is the logical problem of foreign language learning? In S. Gass & J. Schachter (Eds.), *Linguistic perspectives on second language acquisition* (pp. 41–68). New York: Cambridge University Press.

Braunstein, L. (2006). Adult ESL learners' attitudes towards movement (TPR) and drama (TPR storytelling) in the classroom. *CATESOL, 18*(1), 7–20.

Carroll, S., & Swain, M. (1993). Explicit and implicit negative feedback: An empirical study of the learning of linguistic generalization. *Studies in Second Language Acquisition, 15*, 357–386.

Carroll, S., Roberge, Y., & Swain, M. (1992). The role of feedback in second language acquisition: Error correction and morphological generalization. *Applied Psycholinguistics, 13*, 173–198.

Chaudron, C. (1977). A descriptive model of discourse in the corrective treatment of learners' errors. *Language Learning, 27*, 29–46.

Chaudron, C. (1985). Intake: On methods and models for discovering learners' processing of input. *Studies in Second Language Acquisition, 7*, 1–14.

Conrad, D. (2005). Building and maintaining community in cohort-based online learning. *Journal of Distance Education, 20*(1), 1–20.

Corder, S. P. (1967). The significance of learners' errors. *IRAL, 5*, 161–170.

Council of Europe (2009). *Common European Framework of Reference for Languages: Learning, teaching, assessment.* Cambridge, UK: CUP / Council of Europe.

Crouse, D. (2012, October). *Going for 90% plus: How to stay in the target language.* American Council on the Teaching of Foreign Languages. Retrieved from www.actfl.org/sites/default/files/pdfs/TLE_pdf/TLE_Oct12_Article.pdf

Doughty, C. (2001). Instructed SLA: Constraints, compensation, and enhancement. In C. Doughty & M. Long (Eds.), *Handbook of second language acquisition* (pp. 256–310). New York: Blackwell.

Ellis, R. (2003). *Task-based language learning and teaching.* Oxford, UK: Oxford University Press.

Ellis, R. (2006). Current issues in the teaching of grammar: An SLA perspective. *TESOL Quarterly, 40*(1), 83–107.

Ellis, R. (2009). Corrective feedback and teacher development. *L2 Journal, 1*(1), 3–18.

Ellis, R., Basturkmen, H., & Loewen, S. (2001). Leaner uptake in communicative ESL lessons. *Language Learning, 51*, 281–318.

Ellis, R., Sheen, Y., Murakami, M., & Takashima, H. (2008). The effects of focused and unfocused written corrective feedback in an English as a foreign language context. *System, 36*(3), 353–371.

Gass, S. M. (1997). *Input, interaction, and the second language learner.* Mahwah, NJ: Lawrence Elrbaum.

Han, Z-H. (2002). A study of the impact of recasts on tense consistency in L2 output. *TESOL Quarterly, 36*, 543–572.

Harley, B. (1988). Effects of instruction on SLA: Issues and evidence. *Annual Review of Applied Linguistics, 9*, 164–178.

Harrison, R., & Thomas, M. (2009). Identity in online communities: Social networking sites and language learning. *International Journal of Emerging Technologies and Society, 7*(2), 109–124.

Hendrickson, J. (1978). Error correction in foreign language teaching: Recent theory, research, and practice. *Modern Language Journal, 62*, 387–398.

Hsu, H. Y., Wang, S. K., & Comac, L. (2008). Using audioblogs to assist English-language learning: An investigation into student perception. *Computer Assisted Language Learning, 21*(2), 181–198.

James, C. (1998). *Errors in language learning and use.* London & New York: Longman.

Krashen, S. D. (1981). *Second language acquisition and language learning.* Oxford, UK: Pergamon Press.

Krashen, S. D. (1982). *Principles and practice in second language acquisition.* New York: Pergamon Press.

Krashen, S. D. (1985). *The input hypothesis: Issues and implications.* Boston, MA: Addison-Wesley Longman Ltd.

Lightbown, P., & Spada, N. (1990). Focus on form and corrective feedback in communicative language teaching: Effect on second language learning. *Studies in Second Language Acquisition, 12*, 429–448.

Liu, Y. J. (Ed.). (2016). *Authentic materials for Chinese teaching and learning.* Retrieved from www.teach-chinese.com/download/

Long, M. H., Inagaki, S., & Ortega, L. (1998). The role of implicit negative feedback in SLA: Models and recasts in Japanese and Spanish. *The Modern Language Journal, 82*, 357–371.

Lyster, R. (1998). Recasts, repetition, and ambiguity in L2 classroom discourse. *Studies in Second Language Acquisition, 20*, 51–81.

Lyster, R., & Mori, H. (2006). Interactional feedback and instructional counterbalance. *Studies in Second Language Acquisition, 28*, 321–341.

Lyster, R., & Ranta, L. (1997). Corrective feedback and learner uptake: Negotiation form in communicative classrooms. *Studies in Second Language Acquisition, 19*, 37–66.

Oliver, R. (1995). Negative feedback in child NS-NNS conversation. *Studies in Second Language Acquisition, 17*, 459–481.

Oliver, R. (2000). Age differences in negotiation and feedback in classroom and pairwork. *Language Learning, 50*(1), 119–151.

Panova, I., & Lyster, R. (2002). Patterns of corrective feedback and uptake in an adult ESL classroom. *TESOL Quarterly, 36*, 573–595.

Ray, B., & Seely, C. (1998). *Fluency through TPR storytelling: Achieving real language acquisition in school.* Berkeley, CA: Command Performance Language Institute.

Richardson, W. (2006). *Blogs, wikis, podcasts, and other powerful web tools for classrooms.* Thousand Oaks, CA: Corwin Press.

Russell, V. (2009). Corrective feedback, over a decade of research since Lyster and Ranta (1997): Where do we stand today? *Electronic Journal of Foreign Language Teaching, 6*(1), 21–31.

Schmidt, R. (1990). The role of consciousness in second language learning. *Applied Linguistics, 11*, 129–158.

Schwartz, B. D. (1993). On explicit and negative data effecting and affecting competence and linguistic behavior. *Studies in Second Language Acquisition, 15*(2), 147–163.

Sheen, Y. (2006). *Corrective feedback, individual differences, and the acquisition of English articles by second language learners* (Doctoral dissertation, University of Nottingham).

Smith, M. S. (1986). Comprehension versus acquisition: Two ways of processing input. *Applied Linguistics, 7*(3), 239–256.

Smith, M. S. (1991). Speaking to many minds: On the relevance of different types of language information for the L2 learner. *Second Language Research, 7*(2), 118–132.

Spada, N., & Lightbown, P. (1993). Instruction and the development of question in the L2 classroom. *Studies in Second Language Acquisition, 15*, 205–221.

Storch, N. (2010). Critical feedback on written corrective feedback research. *International Journal of English Studies, 10*(2), 29–46.

Sun, Y. C. (2009). Voice blog: An exploratory study of language learning. *Language Learning & Technology, 13*(2), 88–103.

Sung, E., & Mayer, R. E. (2012). Five facets of social presence in online distance education. *Computers in Human Behavior, 28*(5), 1738–1747.

Swain, M. (1985). Communicative competence: Some roles of comprehensible input and comprehensible output in its development. *Input in Second Language Acquisition, 15*, 165–179.

Swain, M. (2005). The output hypothesis: Theory and research. In E. Heinkel (Ed.), *Handbook of research in second language teaching and learning* (vol. 1; pp. 471–483). Abingdon, UK & New York: Routledge.

Swain, M., & Lapkin, S. (1995). Problems in output and the cognitive processes they generate: A step towards second language learning. *Applied Linguistics, 16*(3), 371–391.

Thompson, T. (1997). Do we need to train teachers how to administer praise? Self-worth theory says we do. *Learning and Instruction, 7*, 49–63.

Truscott, J. (1999). The case for "the case for grammar correction in L2 writing classes": A response to Ferris. *Journal of Second Language Writing, 8*, 111–122.

University of Cambridge, ESOL Examinations (2011). *Using the CEFR: Principles of good practice*. Cambridge, UK: Cambridge ESOL.

4 Using technology to promote oral proficiency

Broadly speaking, language proficiency refers to a person's ability to use a language for a variety of purposes and in different modes. Learners at different proficiency levels are able to perform tasks that differ both quantitatively and qualitatively in terms of text[1] length, text type, time framing, and achieved functionality. Both ACTFL Proficiency Guidelines and CEFR have provided detailed descriptions of the parameters/benchmarks for each proficiency level. In order to help learners advance from one level to the next, teachers should carefully design their learning activities to solidify learners' current proficiency and *probe* into the next level by defining the preferred outcome (output), offering comprehensible input, and designing meaningful tasks to facilitate the processing from input to output through interaction. In this chapter and the next, I am going to discuss how technology may enhance our instructional design and help learners achieve higher proficiency. The current chapter will focus on the development of oral proficiency (listening and speaking) and the next will focus on developing literacy (reading and writing). Please note that this division between oral proficiency and literacy is adopted for the convenience of discussion, as technological tools tend to be established to promote one of the two sets of skills. In actual classroom practice, an activity may be and is often composed of tasks that require both oral proficiency and literacy. For instance, learners may be asked to watch a video clip (oral proficiency) and write a reflection (literacy), or to read a menu (literacy) and order from the waiter (oral proficiency) in a role play. Technological tools introduced in this and the next chapters may also be combined whenever appropriate for such integrated activities.

In this chapter, we will discuss the available technological tools, methods, and techniques that may help facilitate learners' development of oral proficiency in Chinese. We will focus on three types of technologies: 1) technologies that help teachers collect and create audio or audiovisual materials, 2) technologies that provide venues and means for various oral communication tasks, and 3) technologies that help learners acquire or improve Chinese pronunciation and intonation.

Technologies for collection/creation of audio(visual) materials

As mentioned in the previous chapter, abundant authentic materials may be found from the Internet, such as streamed videos, podcasts, or live webcasts. I hope you also remember my reminder that in order to select meaningful materials from this seemingly endless supply, we must apply the principle of *i*+1, keeping learners' language proficiency and domain-specific knowledge (including cultural awareness) in mind. This is in fact the biggest challenge for teachers, especially when we teach learners of lower proficiency. One can easily spend hour after hour searching without finding one appropriate clip because such authentic materials are intended for native speakers with a real-life goal and thus tend to include language beyond novice or even intermediate learners' *i*+1 level. While it is not impossible to find sections embedded in raw authentic materials that contain lower-proficiency language, such as a scene of people greeting each other in a movie, it would be extremely time-consuming to attempt to find such clips for every targeted language function. For instance, in order to find authentic language samples of different apologies (e.g. 对不起/對不起, 不好意思, 很抱歉), one may spend many hours watching and filtering videos but still not find appropriate scenes for all of them.

One solution may be using services that offer videos already classified by difficulty levels and themes, such as Yabla (https://chinese.yabla.com) and FluentU (www.fluentu.com/chinese/). The drawback is that such services usually require purchases or paid subscriptions. And although these pay services have done a decent job finding materials for learners of novice high level and above, they are still very limited in their collection of authentic materials for beginners. Some have attempted to remedy this problem by creating so-called "simulated authentic" materials, which are intended for language learners (vis-à-vis native speakers) yet exhibit features that have a high probability of occurrence in genuine acts of communication (Geddes & White, 1978). Take the case of apologies for example: instead of hundreds of hours spent on finding appropriate authentic clips, simulated dialogues for the same functions could be easily acted out and filmed for learning purposes. This method is adopted by some online Chinese lesson providers, such as Growing Up with Chinese (http://cctv.cntv.cn/lm/learningchinese/01/index.shtml, a CCTV series) and Lantern Institute (www.youtube.com/user/MyLanternVideos, a YouTube channel). Yale University also developed their video-based textbook series, *Encounters* (http://encounterschinese.com), using simulated authentic videos.

If you do not find an ideal audiovisual clip that suits your learners' needs, creating a simulated video on your own might be a plausible solution. I have known many teachers, including myself, who create their own learning materials by asking their colleagues, family and friends, or even students to act out a scene for them to record. Nowadays, the recording of videos has been made easier than ever before with mobile devices. It is easy to record with the camera app on your phone or tablet without having to purchase extra equipment or software.

Figure 4.1 Animated video as audiovisual learning material (Practical Chinese)

Another solution enabled by technology is to make videos with animated rather than human characters. An example is the dialogues used in Practical Chinese (https://communicateinchinese.com), as shown in Figure 4.1.

Animated materials provide extra convenience when we do not have access to resources required for an acted-out scene, such as fluent Chinese actors or a proper filming site. Nowadays, animation tools, such as web-based Go!Animate, Powtoon, Animaker, and Nawmal, or mobile apps such as Sock Puppets (iOS only) and Toontastic, provide rich options of characters and background scenes, as well as allowing the characters to move and talk with recorded voices. Some web-based services[2] even offer text-to-speech simulations that allow users to type lines for the AI characters to voice out. An advantage of using text-to-speech is that we do not need to find real voice-actors to speak Chinese for us to record and it provides voices of different ages and genders. However, some disadvantages are that the speech may come out as discernably robotic, and that it may fail to assign the correct pronunciation to heteronyms such as 觉/覺 in 感觉/感覺 [feel] and 睡觉/睡覺 [sleep]. A trick some teachers use is to type a homophone in the text line. For instance, if the computer reads 觉/覺 in 睡觉/睡覺 as "júe," you may type in the line "睡叫" for the AI to pronounce it accurately.

It is relatively easier to find audiovisual materials for learners of intermediate-high and above proficiency. Movies, TV shows, commercials, and live webcasts can all provide rich linguistic and cultural learning opportunities. If you are looking for a collection of materials instead of individual clips, the Chinese-learning sub-channel of CCTV (http://english.cntv.cn/learnchinese/) has quite a few series for intermediate and advanced learners. BBC 中文网/

中文網 also has a page of 视频材料/視頻材料 (Simplified Chinese page: www. bbc.com/zhongwen/simp/media/video; Traditional Chinese page: www.bbc. com/zhongwen/trad/media/video) that provide current news and cultural topics. In 2018, a group of Chinese teachers compiled a user guide for using authentic short videos in Chinese classes: 《短片里的中国/短片裡的中國/ *Understanding China through Video Clips*》(Liu, 2018. Downloadable at www.teach-chinese.com/download/).

If we would like our learners to just focus on the audio input without the visual component, podcasts would be another useful source for oral materials. There are quite a few podcast collections available online for varied proficiency levels. Commercial sites such as ChinesePod (https://chinesepod.com) and Popup Chinese (http://popupchinese.com) have large collections of podcasts catering to learners of different levels. Free resources on the other hand tend to have more concentrated target audience and topics, such as 皮皮妈讲故事/ 皮皮媽講故事[3]   (https://mp.weixin.qq.com/s/JRyfWItfhwJrruxKQ41nqA) for intermediate learners interested in stories and fairy tales, and 美国之音/ 美國之音 [VOA Chinese] (www.voachinese.com) for advanced learners interested in news events. Learning Chinese through Stories (听故事，学中文/ 聽故事，學中文) (www.learningchinesethroughstories.com) is an exception that is both free and has podcasts for varied levels. There are more multimedia story services that present texts, images, and audio readings at the same time; these will be introduced in the next chapter as these services also enhance literacy, while the services mentioned here focus more on listening.

Audio speed is sometimes a concern when choosing listening materials for learners. It is not uncommon for an otherwise appropriate clip to be just too fast for learners to process. If it is a YouTube video, you may easily adjust the speed from 0.25 (slowest) up to two times (fastest) normal speed via the settings menu. If it is a video file, you may use Windows Media Player (Now Playing >> Enhancements >> Play Speed Settings) or QuickTime for Mac (Hold Option key while clicking on rewind button ◄◄) to change the speed of playback. If it is an audio file, you may still use these players to change the speed, or use this online time stretcher: http://onlinetonegenerator.com/time-stretcher.html without making any modification to the original file. The podcast series 慢速中文 Slow Chinese (www.slow-chinese.com) also addresses this concern and keeps the speed of its podcasts to two to three characters per second.

For younger learners, songs or nursery rhymes could also be a valuable source of language input. There are many YouTube channels that provide collections of such materials, such as 碰碰狐 (www.youtube.com/channel/ UCrLO-yoAu4ZTzRSdmWqS53A) and 宝宝巴士/實實巴士 (www.youtube. com/user/babybus1000).

Let's not forget that in addition to language materials, another important source of input in the classroom is the teacher, which is partially why staying in the target language is highly encouraged if not mandated for language teachers. ACTFL, for instance, recommends that teachers remain in the target language as exclusively as possible (90% plus) at all levels of instruction (ACTFL, 2010). Use of technology may make it easier for the instruction to stay in the target language. As a teacher observed, "we've all found that there is very little that needs to be provided in English if you're using visuals and technology" (Crouse, 2012, p. 26). By using presentational technology, including slideshow tools such as PowerPoint, Keynote, and Google Present, and interactive multimedia tools such as Prezi and Thinglink, teachers are able to explain concepts, set up scenarios, and make their instruction much more comprehensible without switching out of the target language.

Technologies for oral communication tasks

In this section, we will discuss another important way in which technology may help enhance language learning, that is, to provide various venues and means for learners to engage in communicative tasks. For the convenience of discussion, the communicative tasks will be divided into three communication modes: interpretive, interpersonal, and presentational. However, please bear in mind that the three modes may be and often are integrated into a larger project that combines tasks of different modes. While it is not the main purpose of this book to introduce the theoretical background and principles of such integration, I would encourage interested readers to look into publications, workshops, or online resources under the topic Integrated Performance Assessment (IPA) if you would like to familiarize yourself with the concept and practice.

Interpretive-mode tasks

After selecting and presenting appropriate audio(visual) materials to the learners at their $i+1$ level, an important next step for teachers is to ensure that this chosen input was indeed comprehended by the learners. While some general insight could be gained through simply observing learners' reaction (e.g., confused facial expressions; nodding, etc.), or asking forthright questions such as "do you understand?", most teachers would probably agree that learners' comprehension could be assessed more reliably if we have learners *demonstrate* to us what they hear and see from the presented material.

Although such comprehension checks may be executed with an oral Q&A or a traditional pen-and-paper quiz/survey without utilizing modern technology, some technological tools may indeed help us to do it more efficiently and effectively. For instance, conducting a live survey with polling technologies after learners watch a short video clip allows us to collect the same amount of information as having them complete a pen-and-paper worksheet, but with two additional advantages:

1. Learners' response is collected, calculated, and sent to the teacher's device with no delay, which allows us to address comprehension gaps

immediately when they are the most present and relevant, and adjust our lesson accordingly (e.g., replaying the part students are confused about; offering explanations or background knowledge, etc.) to maximize learning.

2. Learners may see how their fellow learners respond, if the teacher chooses to present the result on a projected screen. It could provide an opportunity to engage learners in further discussion, especially when the comprehension questions are not limited to "correct" answers. Most polling tools allow the teacher to collect responses anonymously if they would like to minimize peer pressure or performance anxiety.

Simple poll responses in the format of multiple choices could be collected with tools such as Poll Everywhere, Mentimeter, or Plickers. You may even make it a fun and exciting activity using interactive "quiz game" programs such as Kahoot, Quizlet Live, or Quizizz, which will be introduced in more detail in the section on game-based learning in Chapter 7. However, sometimes true understanding of a text may not be fully demonstrated with such restricted-response questions. While such questions generate the fastest return and are therefore valuable for prompt evaluation of learners' understanding, the limited response format fails to solicit data for deeper analysis, reflection, and appreciation of the given text. This is exactly where ACTFL (2012) draws the line between *comprehension* and *interpretation*, with the latter including learners' "understanding from within the cultural mindset or perspective" (p. 7).

Take Disney's video: *Mickey Mouse in the Year of the Dog* (Thomas, 2018) as an example. This short cartoon embeds many semiotics about the Chinese New Year and provides a rich source of cultural analysis and appreciation. After having learners watch this cartoon, we may ask learners to identify as many Chinese cultural elements in it as possible as an interpretive task, which would not fit in a restricted-response format. For such a task, we need more sophisticated live sharing tools, such as Padlet or Lino, to allow learners to post their ideas. Both tools also allow learners to post multimedia content instead of just typed text so audio and video responses may also be shared synchronously. Google Forms or Docs are also used by many teachers to collect more sophisticated responses from learners.

Specific to video-related interpretive tasks, some tools would allow you to embed interactive content into your own videos and even online streamed videos on YouTube or Vimeo, such as Edpuzzle and PlayPosit, which were mentioned in the previous chapter as tools for embedding audio feedback into learners' video-recorded speech. Teachers may use these tools to insert questions into the video at any point (timestamped) for learners to respond to before resuming the video. If you use Camtasia to create videos, it also has a built-in video quiz/survey function but learners will have to use TechSmith Smart Player to view the videos for the quiz/survey to operate properly. Some advantages of using such interactive video tools include:

- The comprehension check does not have to wait until the end of the video. Since questions could be inserted at the time spot where they are the most relevant, it may lessen the burden of memorization and focus more on comprehension.
- The viewing of the video can be self-paced and self-evaluated. Learners may pause and/or re-watch a section to verify their answers to the comprehension questions.
- Learners' responses can be stored for a later analysis or for graded assessment. Both Edpuzzle and PlayPosit may be integrated into learning management systems (LMS) such as Blackboard, Canvas, or Moodle.

Interpersonal-mode tasks

Technological tools for interpersonal and presentational communication tasks overlap to some extent. For instance, a webcam can be used to record a spontaneous, unscripted conversation between two speakers and can also be used to record a scripted and/or rehearsed presentation. For the convenience of discussion, I will introduce the tools that are more commonly used to promote interpersonal communication in this section, and those that are more commonly used for presentational communication in the next. Please note that most of them can also accommodate tasks in the other mode provided there is a different task design.

Tasks of oral interpersonal communication usually involve spontaneous, unscripted, and unrehearsed dialogue between two or more speakers. Unlike interpretive-mode tasks, which emphasize the successful processing of language input, interpersonal tasks tend to place equal emphasis on input (i.e., speakers have to process what they hear from their conversation partners in order to respond appropriately in the conversation) and output (i.e., speakers have to produce language themselves for the conversation to take place).

As mentioned in Chapter 3, one way that technologies help to promote learners' comprehensible output is to simulate real-life situations and thus contextualize the task through images, music/sound, videos, and props, etc. For instance, in a role-play task set in a Chinese restaurant, projecting a restaurant background image on the screen with Chinese songs could help immerse learners in the context; obtaining a menu from a Chinese restaurant via the Internet could provide an authentic prop for the scene.

Technology also makes it easier to connect learners with native speakers. Using conferencing tools, such as Zoom, Adobe Connect, Skype, or Google Hangouts, learners may engage in a casual conversation with native speakers, conduct interviews with them, or have a cross-cultural discussion. If mobile devices are preferred, all these services have developed apps to download on both iOS and Android systems. In addition, there are also many mobile apps, such as FaceTime (iOS), Viber (Android), Facebook Messenger Lite (Android), WhatsApp, WeChat, and LINE, that allow learners to have virtual face-to-face conversations on the phone for free. The major difference between online conferencing tools and live chat apps is that the former can take a larger number of participants and the latter is more suitable for one-on-one conversations.

Among these mobile apps, WeChat and LINE are very popular in China and Taiwan, respectively, which might make it more convenient to connect to native speakers in those local communities. The operational language of these apps can also be set to Chinese easily via "settings," to provide an even more immersive environment.

Of course, these live chat tools are not limited to conversation between learners and native speakers only. We can also easily have our learners talk to one another virtually, which is useful for online courses or the online component of hybrid courses that wish to extend the opportunities for learners' oral communication outside of the classroom. Teachers may also use the conferencing tools to hold their class meetings or office hours online. It could be particularly helpful for teachers who live and work in areas with extreme weather to avoid cancelling an excessive number of class meetings. I have also personally used online meetings when I was out of town attending conferences but did not want to cancel several days of classes in a row.

Some of these tools provide a recording option, which could come in handy for the teacher to review learners' conversations and provide feedback. Among the conferencing services, Zoom and Adobe Connect have built-in recording, and meetings on Google Hangouts can be recorded and automatically saved as a YouTube video if you choose to check the "Enable Hangouts on Air" box when you started the hangout session. However, it is worth mentioning that it would also cause the conversation to be aired live on your YouTube channel and Google+ Stream and viewable to all of your followers. Skype currently only provides a built-in recording option for its paid Skype for Business users, but not for regular free accounts. However, regardless of the conferencing service, you may always use screen-capturing tools to record what happens on your screen, in this case the meeting, as a local video file or a URL link. Several popular screen-capturing tools include Screencast-O-Matic (web-based), ShowMore (web-based), Screencastify (Chrome browser only), Camtasia (Mac and Windows), or QuickTime (Mac). If you use a mobile device for meetings or live chats, you may use apps such as Apowersoft (iOS or Android) or DU Recorder (Android). For iOS devices (iPhone, iPad, or iPod touch) that operate iOS 11, you may also enable Screen Recording through "customize controls" in the Control Center without downloading any external apps.

Although these live conferencing and chatting services feature video calls, all of them also provide audio call options. Another audio-only alternative would be Google Voice. Unlike the other live chat apps mentioned above, one advantage of using Google Voice is that you can get a specific Google Voice number that is different from your personal phone number, and thus may provide more protection of the user's privacy. In order to record a Google Voice call, you need to first enable it through "call options" in the "settings" menu. After it is enabled, you may simply tap "4" any time during a Google Voice conversation on the phone to start and stop the recording. The audio will show up in the user's inbox of their Google Voice account and can be forwarded to others via email or downloaded as an audio file.

Video/audio recording technologies may help oral interpersonal tasks not only in the virtual context, but may provide extra learning opportunities even when the conversation happens in an actual in-person context. Imagine a teacher has their learners paired up and talking about their summer plans with their partner, which is a common setup in a face-to-face classroom. All of the paired-up students then begin to talk simultaneously. While the teacher may walk around and provide assistance and feedback to individual learners, such assistance and feedback is inevitably incidental because it is simply impossible for the teacher to hear the full length of every single conversation, as they all happen at the same time.

Having the interpersonal task recorded may be remedial to this specific problem. As mentioned in Chapter 3, recording learners' language output may help us to combine the advantages of immediate feedback (clear mapping of correction to error) and delayed feedback (uninterrupted communication flow). Not only can we teachers listen to every learner's language output, learners may also listen to their own language use while receiving feedback from us. It is very effective to have such recorded evidence if a teacher plans to have a one-on-one conference with individual learners to evaluate their performance and provide constructive feedback.

Furthermore, such records may be collected over a longer period of time and included in learners' portfolios as evidence of learning to demonstrate progress. It helps the learner to evaluate and plan for their own learning; seeing their own progress motivates them to continue to learn more. Many teachers I have had the pleasure to talk to also simply enjoy filming their students' speeches and performances as accomplishments. Learners tend to appreciate and react positively when they sense their teachers are proud of them.

Nowadays, such in-class recordings can be made very easily with the camera app on mobile devices and shared on the course's learning management system, cloud services (e.g., Google Drive or Dropbox), or via email. Some teachers enjoy the convenience of some video management services such as Flipgrid or Recap. These services allow learners to do a recording with just one click on their device and the upload is automatic. Teachers may also leave comments very easily by responding to each video. Depending on the setting you choose on the service, peer feedback and response is also possible.

Another advantage of recorded language samples is that they are documented learning evidence which can be easily presented to school (district) administrators, parents, and other stakeholders. An app called Seesaw is commonly used for this purpose, in which the teacher has full control over sharing students' work with a selected audience (e.g., individual students, the whole class, or parents). Learners may also create multimedia content (e.g., videos, images, voice narration, drawings and doodles, etc.) directly in this app and share their work while skipping the steps of saving files and uploading, which makes it easier for younger learners to use.

Presentational-mode tasks

As mentioned in Chapter 3, one of the advantages of using instructional technology in a language classroom is that it provides alternative venues for comprehensible output, which allows learners to engage in language activities outside of the physical classroom and thus extends exposure to the target language. This advantage is especially crucial to presentational tasks because such tasks (e.g., storytelling, slideshow presentation, or skits) tend to take up more class time if done in person in the classroom. I would like to stress that this is NOT to say all presentational tasks should be done outside of the class, because having a live audience does help to develop learners' confidence, cultivate a sense of learner community, and provide the opportunity for immediate audience participation and interaction (e.g., asking the presenter questions). The presenters may also observe the audience reaction and adjust their presentation (e.g., providing clarification when observing confusion) in the real-time setting, which is an important skill to learn. What I am saying is that presentational technologies *increase* learners' engagement in presentational tasks by providing alternative venues outside of the classroom, rather than *replacing* the in-person presentation tasks in the classroom.

With this understanding, let's first look at audio tools for simple speech recording tasks, and then move on to tools that accommodate more complicated multimedia presentations. For simple audio recording, learners may use Voice Recorder (Windows), GarageBand (Mac), or Audacity (both Windows and Mac) to achieve the task. Many mobile apps also allow users to record their speech and upload audio files via email or cloud services, such as Audio Recorder (Android), Voice Memos (iOS), or Easy Voice Recorder (Android and iOS). Some web-based services can also be used to collect learners' audio. For instance, Vocaroo allows learners to record and share the audio as a link, which saves them the trouble of uploading or attaching files.

Some more sophisticated tools provide additional functions that could be handy for teachers and learners. For instance, two of the aforementioned services, Recap and Flipgrid, allow learners to record both audio and video speeches with quite easy operation. The former also allows the teacher to have several questions or tasks in "queues" for learners to respond to in a sequenced and progressive manner. For example, if the topic is 你最喜欢的中国饭馆/你最喜歡的中國飯館 (Your Favorite Chinese Restaurant), the queue could be:

1. 你最喜欢的中国饭馆叫什么名字?/你最喜歡的中國飯館叫什麼名字? (What's the name of the restaurant?)
2. 这家饭馆在哪儿? /這家飯館在哪兒? (Where is the restaurant?)

3. 你为什么喜欢这家饭馆？/你為什麼喜歡這家飯館？ (Why do you like this restaurant?)
4. 你常常跟谁去这家饭馆？/你常常跟誰去這家飯館？ (Who do you usually go with to this restaurant?)
5. 请介绍一道你最喜欢的菜。/請介紹一道你最喜歡的菜。 (Please introduce your favorite dish.)

Flipgrid does not have this "queue" function, but it allows learners to record video comments as responses to videos posted by others. For instance, if you have your students record a self-introduction video in Chinese as the initial task, you can then ask each student to video-respond to three classmates with comments on what they share in common (e.g., "我们都喜欢游泳。/ 我們都喜歡游泳。/We both like swimming." "我们都是纽约人。/ 我們都是紐約人。/We're both from New York.").

Another commonly used service, Lingt, currently only records audio but it also provides a queue function similar to Recap. A unique feature is that it can embed and mix multiple types of media in one integrated task. As seen in Figure 4.2, the learner first watches a YouTube video about how to say different dates in Chinese, and then they practice saying the dates corresponding to the image prompts. In the third step, they complete dialogues with the teacher's pre-recorded voice prompts. It is worth noticing that the design of Lingt is more flexible in terms of item sequencing, which means the teacher's recorded prompt does not need to always be the first turn of the conversation. As you may see in Figure 4.2, the last dialogue has the microphone icon (indicating student response) before the audio play icon (indicating voice prompt). Therefore, students need to come up with the question 你妈妈的生日是几月几号？/你媽媽的生日是幾月幾號？ (What is your mom's birthday?) that would lead to the response they hear: 我妈妈的生日是十二月二十号。/ 我媽媽的生日是十二月二十號。 (My mom's birthday is December 20th.)

I categorize such recorded response tasks as presentational although they could appear to be highly conversational. The reasons why they are considered presentational rather than interpersonal are that learners can indeed prepare for and practice their responses, and that they are only responding to pre-recorded prompts, which cannot generate follow-up spontaneous communication. However, although these tasks are presentational themselves, they could help prepare learners to succeed in more spontaneous interpersonal communication in similar contexts and/or with similar topics.

The most valuable contribution technology makes to learners' presentational communication occurs when we move beyond just speech and enter the realm of multi-mode presentations, in which learners use a combination of various semiotics to help them fully express themselves. A very common example is when learners use slideshow technologies (e.g., PowerPoint, Keynote, or Google Slides) to integrate text, images, audios, videos, and/or visual and sound effects with their speech presentation, all of which work together to maximize the comprehensibility and impact of their presentation.

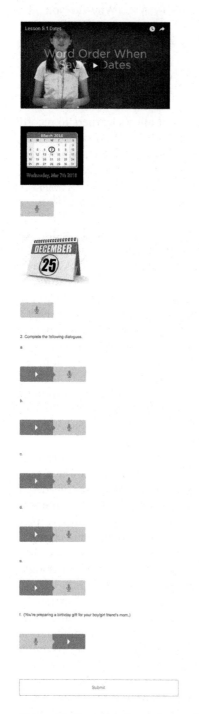

Figure 4.2 Example of an integrated task using Lingt

If learners would like to create a slideshow with recorded instead of live speech, they may use the "record slides" option under "slideshow" in PowerPoint, or "record" under "document > audio" in Keynote. Google Slides does not currently offer built-in recording, but one may always use the aforementioned screen-capturing tools (e.g., Screencast-O-Matic, Screencastify, ShowMore, Camtasia, and QuickTime) to record the presentation externally as a video.

Voicethread, Adobe Spark, Explain Everything, and ShowMe are some other applications that allow learners to create recorded narratives with more creative options. For instance, Voicethread allows multiple learners to record comments on the same image or video; Adobe Spark provides many design options and its one-click recording on the mobile app is easy for even younger learners to use; Explain Everything and ShowMe are both "interactive whiteboard" mobile apps that offer creative tools for graphics, drawing, and doodling. ShowMe and Educreations offer free plans (with limited features), and Explain Everything, while it does not have a free plan, allows multiple users to work on the same presentation collaboratively and simultaneously.

Animation is another form of presentation that allows learners to use language creatively and appeals to the fun factor of language learning. With animation tools, learners may create dialogues in daily scenes such as dining, going to school, dating, or seeing a doctor. They may also create extraordinary situations such as meeting an alien, talking to a historic figure, or living as a fantasy character. Such tasks tend to be highly engaging, individualized, and motivating for learners to fully exploit their language capacity. There are lots of animation tools, with a range of operational complexity, for teachers and learners to choose from. Some of them are more sophisticated and would suit adolescents and adult learners, such as the aforementioned Go!Animate, Powtoon, and Animaker, while some are simpler in design and could be used by much younger children, most of which are mobile apps, such as Toontastic and Sock Puppets.

A reduced version of animation is to just create a single avatar and record voice for it to "talk" with a moving mouth. It could be done using web-based tools such as Voki, or mobile apps such as ChatterPix (iOS) and Telegami. The utilization of such *character talk* may go beyond just a fun activity and involve higher cognitive functions. For instance, we may ask learners to speak on behalf of the earth in a theme unit on environmental protection, or a historical figure such as 武则天/武則天 (Empress Wu) or 孔子 (Confucius). A drawback is that (the free version of) all these services currently have relatively short time limits (30 and 60 seconds maximum, respectively, in their free plans), which does not accommodate speech of longer length. However, some believe that the time limits could encourage learners to be more thoughtful and succinct with their speech.

In addition to animations, skits and short films are also an option for fun and situated comprehensible output in presentational mode. Unedited skits may be recorded easily with the built-in camera on the computer or mobile devices, while a short film (typically with several scenes and some transitional effects) may require basic filming and editing skills, which makes it more appropriate for older learners. iMovie (Mac), Shotcut, Filmora, Video Remix (Windows), and Adobe Spark can perform a great array of basic as well as more sophisticated editing at very low cost or free.

Dubbing is another common presentational activity that situates language use in a simulated real-life context, in which learners create lines and voice-act dialogues that are meaningful to the scene. Dubbing apps are available on mobile devices, such as Dubbing Video Voice (Android), Dubbing (iOS), or DubMe (iOS). These apps allow you to upload your videos and dub over them. 配音秀 is another dubbing app that works differently: Instead of using your own videos, 配音秀 has a large collection of scenes from Chinese TV shows, movies, and commercials that are ready for dubbing. Using this app, one may either dub the scene with the original script, which is conveniently provided in the app, or use the "edit" function to create one's own lines.

Technologies for learning Chinese pronunciation and intonation

Pronunciation might not be placed at the center of a communicative task and many believe that "perfect," native-like pronunciation may not be a reasonable pursuit for foreign language learners after a certain age (see Singleton & Lengyel, 1995 and Moyer, 2004 for the debate over the critical age hypothesis in second language acquisition). However, a certain level of phonological accuracy is still necessary for one's speech to be intelligible and comprehensible to others and should be learned as a component of communicative competence. With Chinese, one particularly important element of pronunciation acquisition is the distinction and production of tones, which could be challenging for learners who are unfamiliar with tonal languages.

While such acquisition may rely heavily on modeling and individual feedback from the teacher, technology may lend a hand for learners' continuous self-practice; this is important to establish procedural memory (a.k.a. muscle memory) that helps learners to produce sounds naturally in speech without constant conscious monitoring, which could overload their cognition and cause undesirable gaps in speech.

For someone who just started learning pinyin and Chinese phonetics, a pinyin chart that contains all Chinese sound combinations could be handy. Learners may click on each sound combination and hear it pronounced on the pinyin webpage of Arch Chinese (www.archchinese.com/chinese_pinyin. html), Yabla (https://chinese.yabla.com/chinese-pinyin-chart.php), and YoYo Chinese (www.yoyochinese.com/chinese-learning-tools/Mandarin-Chinese-pronunciation-lesson/pinyin-chart-table). All three pinyin charts have sound demonstration in all tones. Arch Chinese also lists the characters corresponding to each sound combination, and YoYo Chinese also has videos that demonstrate how to pronounce the initials and finals unfamiliar to Chinese learners.

If one would like to use mobile apps, Pin Pin and ChinesePod Pinyin work both on iOS and Android devices.

For learners to practice and self-assess distinction of tones in Chinese, many websites and mobile apps provide auditory exercises and games, such as BBC Chinese (www.bbc.co.uk/languages/chinese/games/tones.shtml), Pin Pin (mobile app), and Chinese Pinyin Trainer (mobile app).

There are many fewer services available for learners to practice producing sounds themselves. Some teachers simply use voice recognition (voice-to-text) on mobile devices and ask learners to "type" with their voice in messaging or text-note apps. For instance, if learners pronounce the sound "nǐ shì shéi" accurately, the text 你是谁/你是誰 [Who are you] will show up in the app. One may also choose "voice typing" under "tools" to do so in Google Docs, allowing learners to share their results immediately. This option currently only works on Chrome though. With other browsers, you have to set up voice input in the general computer setting (For Mac: System Preferences > Keyboard > Dictation; for Windows: Control Panel > Ease of Access > Speech Recognition). Using this method, users will be able to voice-type in any programs on the computer, not just in Google Docs. Figure 4.3 is an example of typing with voice recognition in Microsoft Word on a Mac computer.

When dealing with tonal languages like Chinese, however, a downside of using voice typing for pronunciation exercise is that this technology aims to *maximize* recognition and thus does not require accuracy in tones. Therefore, we may only use it for general pronunciation practice and save tone exercises for individual face-to-face sessions.

Figure 4.3 Example of voice typing

iSpraak[4] is a web application that takes voice recognition technology one step further for the purpose of language education. It allows the teacher to generate exercises by inputting a text and/or audio file (see Figure 4.4). Learners then record their speech based on the given text/audio and receive automated feedback on the accuracy of their pronunciation. While it provides the convenience of automated feedback, it is worth noting that it still falls short in terms of tone detection because its operation is essentially built on Google's voice recognition technology.

A mobile app called 正音万里行/正音萬里行 (Chinese Sound) seems promising when it comes to helping learners differentiate tones in their language output. In addition to auditory exercises, it has speaking practice in its 汉语拼音方案/漢語拼音方案 (Mandarin Pinyin) section. Learners see a sound represented in pinyin, and hear it in the audio demonstration, and then practice saying it with the correct tone. The system then provides feedback ranging from one to three stars, based on their accuracy of pronunciation. Although the practice is currently limited to individual sounds only, the app does successfully discern different tones the user produces and provided reliable feedback during my testing. The user will receive three stars only when *both* the sound and the tone are accurate. If the sound is correct and the tone is off, they would most likely receive only one star.

In this chapter, we have discussed how technology may assist and enhance the development of oral proficiency, in terms of material selection and creation, oral task design and execution, and tools specific to Chinese

Figure 4.4 Example of a pronunciation exercise on iSpraak
(Reproduced with permission of Dan Nickolai, PhD)

pronunciation and intonation. The next chapter will focus on its counterpart in written communication: the development of literacy and how technology may contribute to it.

Resources

1. Chinese video material services:
   Yabla: https://chinese.yabla.com
   FluentU: www.fluentu.com/chinese/
   Growing Up with Chinese (CCTV series): http://cctv.cntv.cn/lm/ learningchinese/01/index.shtml
   Lantern Institute (YouTube channel): www.youtube.com/user/MyLantern Videos
   Encounters (Video-based textbook): http://encounterschinese.com
   Practical Chinese: https://communicateinchinese.com
   CCTV Chinese Learning Channel: http://english.cntv.cn/learnchinese/
   BBC 中文网 (Simplified Chinese page): www.bbc.com/zhongwen/simp/ media/video
   BBC 中文網 (Traditional Chinese page): www.bbc.com/zhongwen/trad/ media/video
2. Chinese podcast collections:
   ChinesePod: https://chinesepod.com
   Popup Chinese: http://popupchinese.com)
   皮皮妈讲故事 / 皮皮媽講故事: https://mp.weixin.qq.com/s/JRyfWI tfhwJrruxKQ41nqA, (also available via WeChat official account: 亲子微时光 / 親子微時光)
   VOA: 美国之音 / 美國之音: www.voachinese.com
   Learning Chinese through Stories (听故事，学中文 / 聽故事，學中文): www.learningchinesethroughstories.com
   慢速中文 Slow Chinese: www.slow-chinese.com
3. Chinese children song YouTube channels:
   碰碰狐: www.youtube.com/channel/UCrLO-yoAu4ZTzRSdmWqS53A
   宝宝巴士 / 寶寶巴士: www.youtube.com/user/babybus1000
4. Pinyin charts with sound demonstration:
   Arch Chinese: www.archchinese.com/chinese_pinyin.html)
   Yabla: https://chinese.yabla.com/chinese-pinyin-chart.php
   YoYo Chinese: www.yoyochinese.com/chinese-learning-tools/Mandarin-Chinese-pronunciation-lesson/pinyin-chart-table
   Pin Pin (mobile app):
   iOS: https://itunes.apple.com/us/app/pin-pin-free-pinyin-chart-lessons-and-quizzes/id586946693?mt=8
   Android: https://play.google.com/store/apps/details?id=com.zman2245. pinpin
   ChinesePod Pinyin (mobile app):
   iOS: https://itunes.apple.com/us/app/pinyin-by-chinesepod/id833178097? mt=8

  Android: https://play.google.com/store/apps/details?id=com.chinesepod.
   pinyin
5. Auditory tone practice:
  BBC Chinese: www.bbc.co.uk/languages/chinese/games/tones.shtml
  Pin Pin (mobile app):
  iOS: https://itunes.apple.com/us/app/pin-pin-free-pinyin-chart-lessons-
   and-quizzes/id586946693?mt=8
  Android: https://play.google.com/store/apps/details?id=com.zman2245.
   pinpin
  Chinese Pinyin Trainer:
  iOS: https://itunes.apple.com/us/app/pinyin-trainer-by-trainchinese/id3767
   97304?mt=8
  Android: https://play.google.com/store/apps/details?id=com.molatra.piny
   intrainer

Tools

1. Animation tools:

Product Name	GoAnimate
Function	Make animated videos with cartoon characters
Difficulty Level	★★
Product Website	https://goanimate.com/

Product Name	Powtoon
Function	Make animated videos with cartoon characters
Difficulty Level	★★
Product Website	www.powtoon.com/

Product Name	Animaker
Function	Make animated videos with cartoon characters
Difficulty Level	★★
Product Website	www.animaker.com

Product Name	Nawmal
Function	Make animated videos with cartoon characters
Difficulty Level	★★
Product Website	www.nawmal.com

Product Name	Sock Puppets (iOS mobile app)
Function	Make animated videos with sock puppet characters
Difficulty Level	☆
Product Website	https://itunes.apple.com/us/app/sock-puppets/ id394504903?mt=8

Product Name	Toontastic (iOS and Android mobile app)
Function	Make animated videos with cartoon characters
Difficulty Level	★
Product Website	https://toontastic.withgoogle.com

Product Name	Voki
Function	"Avatar"-style cartoon character voice recording
Difficulty Level	☆
Product Website	www.voki.com

Product Name	ChatterPix (iOS)
Function	"Avatar"-style cartoon character voice recording
Difficulty Level	☆
Product Website	https://itunes.apple.com/us/app/chatterpix/id734038526?mt=8

Product Name	Telegami
Function	"Avatar"-style cartoon character voice recording
Difficulty Level	☆
Product Website	https://tellagami.com

2. Video/audio speed-altering players:

Product Name	Windows Media Player (Windows)
Function	Video/audio playback with customized speed
Difficulty Level	☆
Product Website	www.microsoft.com/en-us/download/windows-media-player-details.aspx

Product Name	QuickTime Player (Mac)
Function	Video/audio playback with customized speed
Difficulty Level	☆
Product Website	https://support.apple.com/downloads/quicktime

Product Name	Online Tone Generator
Function	Audio playback with customized speed
Difficulty Level	☆
Product Website	http://onlinetonegenerator.com/time-stretcher.html

3. Live poll tools:

Product Name	Poll Everywhere
Function	Take polls during class presentation and project real-time results
Difficulty Level	☆
Product Website	www.polleverywhere.com

Product Name	Mentimeter
Function	Take polls during class presentation and project real-time results
Difficulty Level	★
Product Website	www.mentimeter.com

Product Name	Plicker
Function	Take polls during class presentation and project real-time results
Difficulty Level	★☆
Product Website	www.plickers.com

4.   Quiz game tools:

Product Name	Kahoot
Function	Quick student responses to questions in a game environment and immediate results
Difficulty Level	★
Product Website	https://kahoot.com/

Product Name	Quizlet Live
Function	Quick student responses to questions in a game environment and immediate results
Difficulty Level	★☆
Product Website	https://quizlet.com/en-gb/features/live

Product Name	Quizizz
Function	Quick student responses to questions in a game environment and immediate results
Difficulty Level	★
Product Website	https://quizizz.com

5.   Tools for live idea posting and sharing:

Product Name	Padlet
Function	Post ideas (including multimedia content) real-time on a shared digital "wall"
Difficulty Level	☆
Product Website	https://padlet.com/

Product Name	Lino
Function	Post ideas (including multimedia content) real-time on a shared digital "wall"
Difficulty Level	☆
Product Website	http://en.linoit.com

Product Name	Google Forms
Function	Collect learner responses in the format of a survey form
Difficulty Level	★
Product Website	www.google.com/forms/about/

Product Name	Google Docs
Function	Real-time text editing by multiple users; can be used to collect feedback from a group of learners
Difficulty Level	☆
Product Website	www.google.com/docs/about/

6. Tools for embedding interactive content in videos:

Product Name	Edpuzzle
Function	Embed interactive content into a video
Difficulty Level	★
Product Website	https://edpuzzle.com/

Product Name	Playposit
Function	Embed interactive content into a video
Difficulty Level	★
Product Website	www.playposit.com

Product Name	Camtasia
Function	Edit videos (including embedding interactive content)
Difficulty Level	Basic recording: ★
	Advanced editing: ★★★
Product Website	www.techsmith.com/video-editor.html

7. Online conferencing tools:

Product Name	Zoom
Function	Have group meetings online
Difficulty Level	★☆
Product Website	www.zoom.us

Product Name	Adobe Connect
Function	Have group meetings online
Difficulty Level	★★★
Product Website	www.adobe.com/products/adobeconnect.html

Product Name	Skype
Function	Have group meetings online
Difficulty Level	★
Product Website	www.skype.com/

Product Name	Google Hangouts
Function	Have group meetings online
Difficulty Level	★☆
Product Website	https://hangouts.google.com

8. Video/audio chat mobile apps:

Product Name	FaceTime (iOS)
Function	Face-to-face video chat
Difficulty Level	☆
Product Website	https://itunes.apple.com/us/app/facetime/id414307850?mt=12

Product Name	Viber (Android)
Function	Face-to-face video chat
Difficulty Level	☆
Product Website	www.viber.com

Product Name	Facebook Messenger Lite (Android)
Function	Face-to-face video chat
Difficulty Level	☆
Product Website	https://play.google.com/store/apps/details?id=com.facebook.mlite

Product Name	WhatsApp
Function	Face-to-face video chat
Difficulty Level	☆
Product Website	www.whatsapp.com

Product Name	WeChat
Function	Face-to-face video chat
Difficulty Level	☆
Product Website	www.wechat.com

Product Name	LINE
Function	Face-to-face video chat
Difficulty Level	☆
Product Website	https://line.me/

Product Name	Google Voice
Function	Have audio chat without using personal phone numbers
Difficulty Level	☆
Product Website	https://voice.google.com/

9. Screen-capturing tools:

Product Name	Screencast-O-Matic
Function	Capture screen activities and audio input on the computer
Difficulty Level	☆
Product Website	https://screencast-o-matic.com

Product Name	ShowMore
Function	Capture screen activities and audio input on the computer
Difficulty Level	★
Product Website	https://showmore.com

Product Name	Screencastify
Function	Capture screen activities and audio input on the computer
Difficulty Level	☆
Product Website	www.screencastify.com

Product Name	Camtasia
Function	Capture screen activities and audio input on the computer
Difficulty Level	Basic recording: ★ Advanced editing: ★★★
Product Website	www.techsmith.com/video-editor.html

Product Name	QuickTime (Mac)
Function	Capture screen activities and audio input on the computer
Difficulty Level	★
Product Website	https://support.apple.com/downloads/quicktime

Product Name	Apowersoft (iOS and Android)
Function	Capture screen activities and audio input on a mobile device
Difficulty Level	★★
Product Website	iOS: www.apowersoft.com/iphone-ipad-recorder Android: www.apowersoft.com/android-recorder

Product Name	DU Recorder (Android)
Function	Capture screen activities and audio input on a mobile device
Difficulty Level	☆
Product Website	https://play.google.com/store/apps/details?id=com.duapps. recorder

Product Name	Screen Recording (iOS)
Function	Capture screen activities and audio input on a mobile device
Difficulty Level	☆
Product Website	Accessible from iOS device's Control Center

10. Video/audio recording and managing services:

Product Name	Flipgrid
Function	Learners record videos in response to prompts; video feedback from the teacher and peers
Difficulty Level	★
Product Website	https://info.flipgrid.com

Product Name	Recap
Function	Learners record videos in response to prompts; can have multiple tasks in a queue
Difficulty Level	★☆
Product Website	https://letsrecap.com

Product Name	Seesaw
Function	Learner- or teacher-recorded videos and other media; allow sharing with selected group members
Difficulty Level	★☆
Product Website	https://web.seesaw.me

Product Name	Lingt
Function	Record learners' audio and text responses; can have multiple tasks in a queue
Difficulty Level	★
Product Website	www.lingt.com

11. Audio recorders:

Product Name	Voice Recorder (Windows)
Function	Record speech audios
Difficulty Level	☆
Product Website	https://info.flipgrid.com

Product Name	GarageBand (Mac)
Function	Record speech and edit audio files
Difficulty Level	Basic recording: ★
	Advanced editing: ★★☆
Product Website	https://letsrecap.com

Product Name	Audacity
Function	Record speech and edit audio files
Difficulty Level	Basic recording: ☆
	Advanced editing: ★★☆
Product Website	www.audacityteam.org

Product Name	Audio Recorder (Andoid)
Function	Record speech audios on mobile devices
Difficulty Level	☆
Product Website	https://play.google.com/store/apps/details?id=com.sonymobile. androidapp.audiorecorder

Product Name	Voice Memos (iOS)
Function	Record speech audios
Difficulty Level	☆
Product Website	Built-in app on iOS mobile devices (accessible on Home Screen, or in "extra" or "utilities" folders depending on the generation)

Product Name	Easy Voice Recorder (iOS and Andoid)
Function	Record speech audios
Difficulty Level	☆
Product Website	iOS: https://itunes.apple.com/us/app/easy-voice-recorder/ id1222784166?mt=8
	Android: https://play.google.com/store/apps/details?id=com. coffeebeanventures.easyvoicerecorder&hl=en

Product Name	Vocaroo
Function	Record speech audios and generate URLs for sharing
Difficulty Level	☆
Product Website	https://vocaroo.com

12. Slideshow technologies:

Product Name	PowerPoint
Function	Create and present slides with option of recorded narration
Difficulty Level	★★
Product Website	https://products.office.com/powerpoint

Product Name	Keynote
Function	Create and present slides with option of recorded narration
Difficulty Level	★★
Product Website	www.apple.com/keynote/

Product Name	Google Slides
Function	Create and present slides with option of recorded narration
Difficulty Level	★★
Product Website	www.google.com/slides/about/

13. Tools for multimedia narratives:

Product Name	Voicethread
Function	Create multimedia narratives; allow for recording from multiple users
Difficulty Level	★★☆
Product Website	https://voicethread.com

Product Name	Adobe Spark
Function	Create multimedia narratives
Difficulty Level	★☆
Product Website	https://spark.adobe.com/

Product Name	Explain Everything
Function	Create multimedia narratives with interactive whiteboard
Difficulty Level	★
Product Website	https://explaineverything.com

Product Name	ShowMe
Function	Create multimedia narratives with interactive whiteboard
Difficulty Level	★
Product Website	www.showme.com

Product Name	Educreations (iOS)
Function	Create multimedia narratives with interactive whiteboard
Difficulty Level	★
Product Website	www.educreations.com

14. Video editing tools:

Product Name	iMovie (Mac only)
Function	Edit videos
Difficulty Level	Basic recording: ★
	Advanced editing: ★★☆
Product Website	www.apple.com/imovie/

Product Name	Shotcut
Function	Edit videos
Difficulty Level	Basic recording: ★
	Advanced editing: ★★
Product Website	www.shotcut.org

Product Name	Filmora
Function	Edit videos
Difficulty Level	★☆
Product Website	https://filmora.wondershare.net/filmora-video-editor.html

Product Name	Video Remix (Windows)
Function	Record and edit videos, photos, and 3-D animations
Difficulty Level	★☆
Product Website	Accessible via Microsoft "Photos" app
	https://support.microsoft.com/en-us/help/17205/ windows-10-create-videos

Product Name	Adobe Spark
Function	Record and edit videos, photos, and webpages
Difficulty Level	★☆
Product Website	https://spark.adobe.com/

Product Name	Camtasia
Function	Edit videos
Difficulty Level	Basic recording: ★
	Advanced editing: ★★★
Product Website	www.techsmith.com/video-editor.html

15. Dubbing mobile apps:

Product Name	Dubbing Video Voice (Android)
Function	Dub videos
Difficulty Level	★
Product Website	https://play.google.com/store/apps/details?id=com. goldenheavan.videovoicedubbing

Product Name	Dubbing (iOS)
Function	Dub videos
Difficulty Level	★
Product Website	https://itunes.apple.com/us/app/dubbing/id564619577?mt=8

Product Name	DubMe (iOS)
Function	Dub videos
Difficulty Level	★
Product Website	https://itunes.apple.com/us/app/dubme-voice-over-videos/id704528400?mt=8

Product Name	配音秀
Function	Dub videos
Difficulty Level	★
Product Website	www.peiyinxiu.com

16. Tools for pronunciation/intonation automated feedback:

Product Name	iSpraak (Chrome browser only)
Function	Assess learners' pronunciation with input prompts by the teacher
Difficulty Level	☆
Product Website	www.ispraak.com

Product Name	正音万里行 / 正音萬里行 (mobile app)
Function	Assess learners' tone production
Difficulty Level	☆
Product Website	www.hschinese.com/zh-hans/app/intro/talk

Notes

1 In second language acquisition, "text" is not limited to written text. It refers to the meaningful language generated by users, which could be either spoken or written.
2 As of Oct. 9, 2017, Go!Animate is the only service that I am aware of that offers this function in Chinese. Nawmal has this function but has not included Chinese yet.
3 The podcasts in 皮皮妈讲故事/皮皮媽講故事 are authentic materials made for native-speaking Chinese children, but the level is suitable for learners of intermediate proficiency and above.
4 iSpraak currently only works on the Google Chrome browser.

References

American Council on the Teaching of Foreign Languages (ACTFL) (2010). *Use of the target language in the classroom*. Retrieved from www.actfl.org/news/position-statements/use-the-target-language-the-classroom

American Council on the Teaching of Foreign Languages (ACTFL) (2012). *Performance descriptors for language learners*. Retrieved from www.actfl.org/sites/default/files/pdfs/ACTFLPerformance_Descriptors.pdf

Geddes, M., & White, R. (1978). The use of semi-scripted simulated authentic speech in listening comprehension. *Audiovisual Language Journal, 16*(3), 137–45.

Liu, Y. J. (Ed.). (2018). *Understanding China through video clips*. Retrieved from www.teach-chinese.com/download/

Moyer, A. (2004). *Age, accent, and experience in second language acquisition: An integrated approach to critical period inquiry* (Vol. 7). Bristol, UK: Multilingual Matters.

Singleton, D. M., & Lengyel, Z. (Eds.). (1995). *The age factor in second language acquisition: A critical look at the critical period hypothesis*. Bristol, UK: Multilingual Matters.

Thomas, D. (Director). (2018, February 10). *Year of the dog*. In P. Rudish (Producer), Mickey Mouse. Disney Channel.

5 Using technology to promote literacy

Oral and written communication may differ in form, but the interactive processing model and the main factors that support the processing remain the same. As mentioned in Chapter 3, in order to facilitate language acquisition, teachers may:

- Provide abundant, authentic, and comprehensible input.
- Raise attention and create environments supporting processing.
- Push for comprehensible output.
- Provide consistent, focused, intense, and individualized feedback.

Keeping these principles in mind, this chapter will focus on how to use technology to develop literacy in the following areas:

- Accessing reading materials.
- Making the reading process observable.
- Creating engaging writing tasks and projects.
- Easy feedback and tracking of multi-draft writing.
- Peer response and collaborative writing.
- Para-literacy tools and exercises.
- Developing digital literacy.

Accessing reading materials

Similar to the development of oral proficiency, exposure to abundant, authentic, and comprehensible input is crucial for developing literacy. Access to such input has been made easier by the infinite reading materials we may find via the Internet. These reading materials are not limited to texts in the form of articles, but may also include posts and comments, comic strips, memes, posters, email correspondence, instant messaging, etc. Even for novice learners whose text types are limited to isolated words and formulaic sentences, there are many types of reading materials (e.g., street names, bus schedules, banners, maps, store hours, or menus) for them to decipher meanings and make connections to the written form of the language. Such materials may easily be found via a keyword search of images on search engines such as Google, Yahoo,[1] or 百度 (Baidu.com).

Intermediate learners may attempt to read short stories, short essays, comic strips, or functional writings (e.g., email messages, notes, etc.) on familiar topics, with the aid of provided vocabulary lists or dictionaries. To this end, technology may facilitate the development of reading proficiency by 1) enabling access to more (variety of) texts, and 2) providing easy-to-access vocabulary lists or online dictionaries. In this section I will focus on sources of texts and save the vocabulary tools for the later section on para-literacy tools.

Compiled collections of short readings for Chinese language learners can be found on many websites such as Mandarin for Me (http://mandarinforme. com/chinese-reading-practice), Learn Mandarin from Chinese Stories (http:// edu.chinese-stories.com), Little Fox Chinese (https://chinese.littlefox.com/ en/story), Chinese Reading Practice (http://chinesereadingpractice.com), or iChineseReaders (https://ichinesereader.com), as well as mobile apps such as Chinese Stories, Decipher Chinese, or Du Chinese. If one feels like using authentic lesson texts that are currently used in elementary and middle schools in China, the website 好爸爸 (www.goodfather.com.cn/index.html) has a collection of digital 语文/語文 [Chinese Study] textbooks by different publishers in China.

An infinite number of authentic Chinese texts may also be found in self-publication networks of Chinese authors such as 短美文网/短美文網 (www. duanmeiwen.com) or 一品故事网/一品故事網 (www.07938.com). These networks usually divide their collections by genre or theme instead of language proficiency levels. Therefore, the teacher's filtering and selecting effort is required when in search of comprehensible materials for their learners.

Learners at advanced proficiency level and above are able to read about subject matters that are new to them *independently*. Generally speaking, the difference among advanced, superior, and distinguished learners lies in 1) the variety of genres. For instance, advanced learners are able to read narrative, descriptive, and straightforward argumentative texts while superior/ distinguished learners are able to read professional, academic, or literary texts; 2) the extent of abstraction and cultural references they are able to discern and understand. Advanced readers tend to still have difficulty comprehending abstract concepts in reading; superior readers may not fully understand texts with cultural references and assumptions deeply embedded in the text; distinguished readers are able to handle a high level of abstraction, density, complexity, nuance, and subtlety in a text. More detailed description of each level and sub-levels may be found in the ACTFL Proficiency Guidelines.

When teaching learners of higher proficiency, the selection of reading texts must cover a wider range of genres and topics and reflect a degree of complexity and abstraction appropriate to the learners' level. Many programs have specialized courses for these learners, such as News Chinese, Chinese Literature, Academic Chinese, or Chinese for Professional Purposes, just to name a few. Therefore, the acquisition of texts in the targeted subject domain should also be taken into consideration. For instance, for News Chinese or courses related to the current political, economic, and social reality of China, news websites would be an appropriate source of texts. It is worth pointing out that since learners of higher proficiency are better capable of detecting and analyzing the writer's intention, multiple news articles on the same topic from different sources and with different perspectives may be very effective materials for critical reading. Some commonly used Chinese news media include:

- News media publishing originally in Chinese:
  人民日报/人民日報: http://paper.people.com.cn (China)
  南方周末: www.infzm.com (China)
  自由时报/自由時報: www.ltn.com.tw (Taiwan)
  苹果日报/蘋果日報: http://hk.apple.nextmedia.com (Hong Kong)
  联合早报/聯合早報: www.zaobao.com.sg (Singapore)
- Global news media that have Chinese editions:
  纽约时报/紐約時報: http://cn.nytimes.com
  华尔街日报/華爾街日報: http://cn.wsj.com/gb/index.asp
  BBC 中文网/BBC中文網: www.bbc.com/zhongwen/simp
  德国之声/德國之聲: www.dw.com/zh
  全球之声/全球之聲: https://zhs.globalvoices.org

The Chairman's Bao (www.thechairmansbao.com) has articles based on news but adapted to accommodate learners of all levels, not just advanced learners.

In addition to news media, the aforementioned self-publication networks (e.g., 短美文网/短美文網 and 一品故事网/一品故事網) have a variety of genres and topics to choose from for advanced learners; 中文阅读天地/中文閱讀天地 (The Chinese Reading World) by the University of Iowa also offers readings and exercises at advanced level. For more specific purposes, 第一文库网/第一文庫網 (www.wenku1.com/list/ 商务合同范本/) and 省心范文网/省心範文網 (www.shengxin118.com) have large collections of business contracts; 法律快车合同范本/法律快車合同範本 (http://fanben. lawtime.cn/jishu/) has law documents; 中国国际剧本网/中國國際劇本網 (www.juben108.com) has both original plays and famous movie/TV/commercial/stage drama scripts; 论文网/論文網 (www.lunwendata.com) and 中国知网/中國知網 (www.cnki.net) provide access to academic publications.

Making the reading process observable

It is worth keeping in mind when designing reading activities that multiple strategies tend to be adopted by successful readers. Brown and colleagues (Brown, Palincsar, & Armbruster, 1984; Palincsar & Brown, 1986) have identified four reading strategies that help readers comprehend meaning from the text:

- Questioning: Readers monitor and assess their comprehension by asking themselves questions to identify information, themes, and important ideas in the text.
- Clarifying: Readers identify and clarify unclear, difficult, or unfamiliar vocabulary, sentence structure, or concepts in the text.
- Summarizing: Readers integrate the acquired information, themes, and ideas into clear and concise statements that communicate the essential meaning of the text. Summarization may occur after reading a sentence, a paragraph, or the whole text.
- Predicting: Readers form and test hypotheses by combining readers' prior knowledge, new knowledge from the text (gained from applying the three strategies mentioned above), and the structure of the text.

Quite compatible to these strategies, the strategies Hosenfeld (1977) found that were adopted by successful L2 readers in particular include: keeping the meaning of the passage in mind while reading, reading in broader phrases, and skipping inconsequential or less important words rather than pondering over them. In order to help learners develop learning strategies and read effectively, a teacher could 1) help learners situate themselves with the overall purpose and context of reading, 2) invite them to constantly ask questions, summarize, and make predictions along the process of reading, and 3) supply clarification clues or explanations to help them comprehend the text.

One challenge language teachers face when teaching reading is that when learners read, the process is obscure and therefore it is hard to observe what strategies they adopt. When conducting studies on reading strategies, researchers often use the "think aloud" technique, asking the individual subject to verbally state what goes on in their mind during reading. While this method is effective for gaining insight into the reading strategies used, it is extremely time-consuming and impractical for teachers to use with individual learners on any regular basis. A more practical alternative that technology provides is for learners to do *annotated reading*. Using word-processing tools such as Microsoft Word, TextEdit, OpenOffice, or Google Docs, learners may highlight important information and unfamiliar phrases/structures/concepts, ask questions, and make comments related to their own experience and prior knowledge, etc. The annotated text may then be shared with the teacher as printouts or via cloud services (e.g. Google Drive, Dropbox, iCloud, or OneDrive). This allows the teacher to observe the thinking process of each learner, assess comprehension, and identify knowledge gaps (as highlighted unfamiliar areas or posted questions) and design further learning experiences accordingly. Annotated reading may also be used creatively with guided questions posted before the reading, and/or comprehension questions or summarizing/predicting tasks at the end.

Annotated reading can be further expanded into *digital social reading*. Social reading existed long before the digital age, mostly in the form of reading groups and discussions. During social reading, learners share reactions to the text, ask and answer questions, provide interpretive and appreciative comments, and discuss cultural phenomena related to the text. Current technology extends such activities beyond the classroom and allows learners to interact virtually over the Internet.

As defined by Blyth (2014), digital social reading is "the act of sharing one's thoughts about a text with the help of tools such as social media networks and collaborative annotation" (p. 205). Some common platforms used for social reading include Google Docs, eComma (University of Texas at Austin), eMargin (Birmingham City University), and Classroom Salon (Carnegie Mellon University).[2] Each platform features some different functions in addition to the shared annotation. Some of them allow for color tagging, some have built-in word clouds, some of them are easy to integrate into certain LMSs, and some provide options for audio or video comments, for example. It will depend on the teacher and learners' needs to decide which platform is the most helpful for them.

Figure 5.1 demonstrates how a social reading task looks in Google Docs. As in annotated reading, learners comment wherever they have questions, opinions, thoughts, and reflections. The main difference between annotated reading and digital social reading is that for the latter, learners address each other's comments by answering others' questions or starting/contributing to a discussion thread.

Studies have shown that learners develop deeper comprehension and more effective reading strategies through social reading/collaborative annotation in both face-to-face settings (Vaughn, Klingner, & Bryant, 2001; Zoghi,

Figure 5.1 Digital social reading example using Google Docs
(Contributor: Hsin-wei Su, Wheaton College)

Figure 5.2 Annotating a webpage (blog) using Hypothes.is

Mustapha, Maasum, & Mohd, 2010) and online contexts (Yang, Zhang, Su, & Tsai, 2011; Chang & Hsu, 2011; Blyth, 2014). Compared to individual annotated reading, social reading allows learners to: 1) co-construct meaning of the text, 2) model after others' reading strategies, and 3) enhance the learner community through interaction.

To extend the practice of social reading from word text to web content, webpage annotation tools such as Hypothes.is (https://web.hypothes.is) or zipBoard (https://zipboard.co) could be helpful. Such tools allow multiple users to annotate a webpage in a similar manner they do text documents. Figure 5.2 is an example of such annotation.

Create engaging writing tasks and projects

Learners can learn to write in Chinese without using technology, but some technologies may help making the writing tasks more enjoyable and engaging for learners. In this section, we are going to look at technological tools that allow learners to create various text forms that involve writing: memes, comic strips, story books, and multimedia publications.

First, let's look at memes. Memes are typically composed of an image with clever captions to convey and spread a message. Such a form of communication is widespread, particularly on social media. Given that the captions tend to be short and simple, even novice learners can enjoy making memes with great originality. Some online tools suitable for such tasks include Meme Generator (https://memegenerator.net), Rage Maker (http://ragemaker.net),

Imgflip (https://imgflip.com/memegenerator), and Canva (www.canva.com). While the former three are more limited to meme creation and thus characteristic of simple operation, Canva is capable of more sophisticated designs for print media (e.g., flyer, posters, invitation cards, and brochures, etc.) and can be used for purposes other than memes.

Taking the concept of writing and creating for fun one step further, we may have learners produce comic strips as a writing project. Online services such as Pixton (www.pixton.com), Toondoo (www.toondoo.com), Make Beliefs Comix (www.makebeliefscomix.com), and StoryboardThat (www.storyboardthat.com) provide users with a wide variety of cartoon characters, scene backgrounds, and items to produce interesting comic stories.

Due to the complexity of operation, these tools are more appropriate for teenage or older learners. Younger learners will most likely need help from adults to use these tools.

There are two other unique tools that fall in the similar writing-for-fun category as memes and comic strips. One is a Chinese web app: 对话泡泡产生器/對話泡泡產生器 (http://make.spotlights.news/bubble/) which allows users to create mock-up text messages between imaginary users (see Figure 5.3 for an example).

Similarly, an online content generator called "fakebook" (www.classtools.net/FB/home-page) allows users to create a fake Facebook wall mock-up with an imaginary profile. In addition to just doing it as a fun activity, a fakebook writing assignment could also be made a research project. For instance, making a fakebook page for the famous poet 李白 (Li Bo) in the Tang Dynasty would require finding who he was friends with, who were in his

Figure 5.3 Example of a mock-up text-messaging conversation using 对话泡泡产生器/對話泡泡產生器

family, what his interests were, and what he would have posted about his life if he had had a Facebook account back then.

A shared characteristic of these tools and tasks is that the writing element in them tends to be relatively short and highly conversational. With progression of learners' proficiency, we may need technological tools that would accommodate longer writing in paragraph forms. Storybook creator sites might provide what we need for such writing projects. Storybird (https://storybird.com) and Book Creator (https://bookcreator.com) are two popular websites that allow learners to create their own visual books with text and illustrations. While such "books" (paragraph texts with accompanying images) may also be created using presentational programs (e.g., PowerPoint, Keynote, or Google Slides) or word processors (e.g., Microsoft Word, Pages, or Google Docs), these creators do provide more appealing designs, ready-for-use illustrations, and convenient storing and sharing options.

Flipsnack (www.flipsnack.com), FlippingBook (https://flippingbook.com), and Joomag (www.joomag.com) are other options for making e-books. Compared to Storybird and Book Creator, this set of tools is more suitable for adult users and more magazine-like publications.

I would like to also mention StoryBoard, a mobile app that is currently only available on Android, which is not a writing tool itself, but may add a more personal touch to the learners' stories. This app films videos using the camera on one's phone and then transforms them into series of images (see Figure 5.4 for example), with many artistic styles to choose from. Such images could be very powerful when used in combination with book creators to tell a personal story.

These book or storyboard projects of learners' personal narratives can be categorized as one type of *digital storytelling*. However, to fully harness its potential educational gain requires not only assigning the projects to learners but careful design and scaffolding in the *process* of composing such digital stories. We will discuss digital storytelling as a unique method of learner-centered language instruction in the next chapter.

Easy feedback and tracking of multi-draft writing

In a similar manner to tracking learners' progress in oral communication and providing feedback, learners' writing may also be tracked and commented on with more efficiency via technology, particularly in the case of multi-draft writing, one of the most commonly adopted methods of L2 writing.

Most SLA scholars recognize the value of multi-draft writing in developing L2 writing proficiency, largely because it encourages learners to incorporate the feedback received between the first and the final drafts, although researchers do differ in what types (e.g., form-oriented or content-oriented feedback) and in what manner feedback should be given (e.g., oral vs. written comment). The incorporation of feedback into later drafts results in both an improved final product and newly established writing strategies (Ferris,

Figure 5.4 Example of images generated with Storyboard

1995; Paulus, 1999); learners also value and expect to learn from the feedback they receive from the teacher between drafts (Cohen & Cavalcanti, 1990; Leki, 1991; Hedgcock & Lefkowitz, 1994; Hyland, 1998; Lee, 2004).

The comment function in word-processing programs (e.g., Word or OpenOffice for offline personal writing; Google Docs or Word through OneDrive for online shared documents) allows teachers to highlight sections of text and add focused feedback to it fairly easily, and learners can make changes directly in the same document while visually seeing the comments in front of them. The revision tracking function allows the teacher to conveniently see the changes individual learners make in the newer draft and assess whether they have successfully incorporated the feedback received earlier in their edits.

Technology also provides the option of leaving audio or even video comments to learners' writing. For instance, in a Microsoft Word document, you may use "insert voice" (for Windows) or "audio notes" (for Mac, which only works in "notebook layout" under the "view" menu) to add a voice comment; on Google Drive, you may use the "connect more apps" function to add "voice comments" (developed by 121 Writing) or use "get add-ons" to get Kaizena Shortcut, either of which would allow you to highlight a section of the text and record your voice as a comment with one click. Students in turn may respond to your comments with voice recording, which may serve as an asynchronous alternative to face-to-face conferencing about their writing.

Peer response and collaborative writing

It is worth noting that such document sharing and commenting is not limited to between the teacher and individual learners. It also accommodates peer response and collaborative writing among learners themselves.

Peer response refers to peer editing and/or commenting, which tends to occur after a draft is completed by an individual learner. Similar to teacher feedback, peer response can easily be implemented, compared, and tracked in a digital environment. Studies have shown that although learners perceive teacher feedback as more informative and of higher quality, they do incorporate both teacher feedback and peer response into their revisions and result in overall improvement of writing (Villamil & Guerrero, 1998; Paulus, 1999; Tsui & Ng, 2000; Hansen & Liu, 2005; Storch, 2005). In addition to being complementary to teacher feedback, peer response may benefit the author in that: 1) It helps create a readership for the writing and raises the author's awareness of the expectations of the intended reader; 2) peer support has a positive affective impact on the author's attitude towards writing in general; and 3) most importantly, during the process of editing and commenting others' work, learners learn to self-edit their own writing more effectively and thus become better writers themselves (Chaudron, 1984; Keh, 1990; Arndt, 1993; Lockhart & Ng, 1993; Rollinson, 2005). Liu and Sadler (2003) compared the effect of online peer review and traditional face-to-face conferencing and found that the quantity of peer comments and consequently the numbers of revisions the author made exceeds those made in face-to-face contexts. However, they also pointed out that the communication between authors and editors was more effective face to face and suggested a two-step review procedure of electronic peer response followed by face-to-face communication for best effect.

Peer response may be part of collaborative writing, but typically collaborative writing calls for more collaboration among learners than simply incorporating others' comments. An important difference is that collaborative writing produces *one single text* with shared responsibility in decision-making processes by multiple authors in *all stages of writing*: planning, generating ideas, deliberation about text structure, editing, and revision (Ede & Lunsford, 1990; Storch, 2013).

A typical procedure of collaborative writing may contain the following steps, with variation depending on the teacher's design:

1. Group forming
2. Brainstorming ideas
3. Coordinating meeting schedules
4. Researching
5. Exchanging information gathered from the research
6. Outlining and planning the content
7. Crafting the first draft
8. Reviewing and editing
9. Repeating some steps for a second/final draft

Technology makes collaborative writing easier in the sense that:

- The text can be shared, drafted, and edited synchronously. Using cloud services for document sharing, co-authors may work on the text at the same time rather than passing it from one person to another and spending most of their time waiting.
- Meetings can be held virtually via video conferencing or text chat, which saves the co-authors the trouble of commuting to be physically in one space. Meetings conducted online can also be saved for record-keeping. Interactive whiteboards such as Explain Everything (mobile app) and the web-based AWW board (https://awwapp.com) enable learners to type, draw, and doodle synchronously, and could help them brainstorm ideas collaboratively.
- Technology makes it easier to collect and share information. Websites, online articles, and media files/links can all be obtained and shared digitally among co-authors.
- The teacher is able to monitor progress during learners' writing process and provide timely guidance, rather than after the draft has already been completed and turned in.

In terms of the actual choice of platform to host learners' collaborative writing, some teachers prefer document sharing tools (e.g., Google Docs or OneDrive) and some prefer wiki sites (e.g., Wikidot, PBworks, or Mediawiki).[3] Google Sites also has wiki templates available for users to create a webpage as a co-edited wiki. As Penna and Fallik (2009) put it in a conference talk, the main difference between the use of Google Docs and a wiki is that they induce different mindsets for users. If you use a document sharing tool like Google Docs, you are creating a text document and the writing and reading experience created in this environment is basically linear, similar to a traditional article. Wikis on the other hand generate webpages, which naturally encourages users to embed multiple media and link to other web resources. The writing and reading experience is thus less linear and more like a cluster or map of content. Another difference is that document-sharing tools are better equipped for synchronous editing, while wikis are more suitable for asynchronous editing. In terms of required technological competence, while both are relatively easy to use, most people find document sharing easier because of the prior familiarization with offline word-processing tools. The operation of wikis does require a slightly higher level of technical savviness, mainly because it allows users to do more with styling, media embedding, linking, and referencing.

Collaborative writing benefits learners in many ways, such as polishing their thinking process, utilizing their social and organizational skills, giving and receiving feedback that helps develop the writer's awareness of readers' expectations, learning writing strategies from one another, drawing attention to syntactic and structural elements of the text, and enhancing learners' motivation to communicate in the target language (Reither & Vipond, 1989; Reid, 1993; Villamil & De Guerrero, 1996; Foster, 1998; Gousseva-Goodwin, 2000; Hansen & Liu, 2005). However, it is worth mentioning that simply asking learners to collaborate is not sufficient to generate such benefits. Storch (2002) and Li and Zhu (2017) have pointed out that only *true collaboration*, which means interaction that exhibits collaborative patterns (as opposed to dominant patterns or sheer division of work that lacks interaction) may generate better writing outcomes and learning uptake. Watanabe (2008) further pointed out that even mixed-level (higher and lower proficiency) peers may contribute to each other's learning as long as they work in a collaborative manner, i.e., sharing many ideas and contributing equally to the writing. From the teacher's perspective, learners' interaction patterns may be more easily monitored in digital collaborative writing through tracking and records of discussion. Examples can also be drawn from learners' recorded communication to demonstrate preferred interaction patterns as models.

Para-literacy tools and exercises

In addition to the technology that is directly used to create reading and writing tasks, there are also tools to help learners develop important skills and knowledge that contribute to reading and writing, including: 1) Tools that help learners look up words and concepts during reading, 2) tools that help to memorize vocabulary, 3) tools that help learners practice connecting ideas/sentences, and 4) tools that help practice character writing. In the following sections, I will introduce several tools and practices in each category:

1. Tools that help learners to look up words and concepts during reading

While successful readers read for meaning in broader phrases rather than stopping and pondering over every unfamiliar word, as mentioned earlier in this chapter, there are times when some unfamiliar words appear to be crucial to interpreting a text and their meaning cannot be inferred easily using contextual clues. When encountering situations like this, a dictionary is one of the first and foremost tools that come to mind for many of us.

With modern technology, learners now have the option of using dictionaries on their computer or mobile devices, as an alternative to traditional print dictionaries. There are a few advantages that online dictionaries offer over print:

- They do not require learners to carry the weight of a big print dictionary, which makes them convenient to use anywhere and any time.
- It easier to input information for search. With a traditional dictionary, learners have to find the page that lists the character/word using a radical or phonetic index, which may take some guesswork since the character/word is unfamiliar to the learner. Online dictionaries allow learners to copy and paste from the original text, if it's digital, and the search work is done automatically after that. If the text is not digital, many online or mobile dictionaries allow learners to input the characters by drawing them using the mouse or touchscreen. This is helpful, particularly when the learner has little orthographic or phonetic information about the character/word they want to look up.
- The content of online dictionaries is up to date and includes the newest entries, while one has to purchase new editions of traditional dictionaries when new entries are added.
- Online/mobile dictionaries often have additional functions that promote learning, such as animated stroke order demonstration, or audio pronunciation.
- Online/mobile dictionaries are often free of cost.

This is not to say that print dictionaries are necessarily inferior to digital ones. For instance, the "inconvenient" factor that requires learners to make guesses about the unfamiliar character's radical or pronunciation in order to look it up may actually force learners to practice and apply their linguistic knowledge and help with retention; when they look up one word in a Chinese print dictionary, they also see other word entries on the same page with the same initial character, which may deepen and expand their semantic knowledge as well. While both print and digital options have unique advantages, learners' needs and preferences should be taken into consideration and it might be beneficial to teach them to use both.

Several commonly used online Chinese-English dictionaries include: YellowBridge (www.yellowbridge.com), MDBG (www.mdbg.net), and LINE (http://ce.linedict.com). Each of them also has extra functions beyond just the meaning of words/characters. For instance, YellowBridge has an etymology tab that gives information on a character's formation method and the meaning and origin of its components; MDBG has a color-coded tone presentation and stroke order demonstration; LINE has a large collection of web-based sample sentences to go with each word. All of them also have audio pronunciation that traditional dictionaries do not provide.

Compared to online dictionaries, mobile dictionaries might not provide as much information yet they offer quick access to the most prominent meanings of a word/character *at a glance* and can be used offline. Two popular mobile apps are Written Chinese and Pleco. Compared to traditional dictionaries, most online and mobile dictionaries have additional functions such as word games, flashcards, corpus examples, or stroke order animations.

For advanced learners, the use of Chinese-Chinese dictionaries may provide more language input and deeper understanding of the etymology and cultural references related to the word. Here are some options if one is looking for Chinese-Chinese dictionaries. Three popular dictionary websites are 汉典/漢典 (www.zdic.net), 萌典 (www.moedict.tw), and 百度词典/百度辭典 (https://dict.baidu.com). For mobile devices, many users choose 新华字典/新華字典[4] or 百度汉语/百度漢語.

While browsing webpages, pop-up Chinese dictionaries may come in handy. Such dictionaries take the form of add-ons or extensions to browsers and show brief definitions when you hover your mouse over Chinese words. Some commonly used ones include: Zhongwen and Perapera for Chrome and Firefox, and Frill for Safari. While such tools provide tremendous convenience, it might be worth reminding learners to use them with caution because having English definitions available for every word in front of them may result in comprehending the whole text in English rather than in Chinese. Having such easy access to definitions of every unfamiliar word might also discourage learners from making inferences on their own based on context, which is important for the development of vocabulary and reading proficiency.

While dictionaries provide large and broad databases of word definitions, sometimes the information may be too overwhelming, especially for novice learners. For instance, even the basic word 好 has many meanings and uses from "good" to "easy," to cheers, greetings, and to a complement marking the completed state of an action, just to name a few. Therefore, it may sometimes be more helpful to provide learners with a vocabulary list with definitions specific to a given text, or a glossary of a certain subject domain. Several tools may help generate such lists, such as the Chinese Vocab List Creator by Arch Chinese (www.archchinese.com/chinese_vocab_list_creator.html) or Vocabulary List Generator by Purple Culture (www.purpleculture.net/vocabulary-list-generator). Both tools allow for customized editing for word definitions, either through live editing when generating the list on their website (the former), or after downloading the list as a .csv excel file.

Also related to vocabulary learning, a unique and interesting set of "dictionaries" has just emerged on the horizon. Using augmented reality (AR) and object identification (OID) technology, some apps allow the learner to scan their environment with the camera on their mobile device and display the name of the scanned item on the screen. Currently available apps that perform this function include: Memrise (iOS) and 百度翻译/百度翻譯 [Baidu Translate] (iOS and Android).

2. Tools that help to memorize vocabulary

Although it is generally agreed by SLA scholars that vocabulary is best acquired through exposure to and inference from contextualized, authentic, and comprehensible input,[5] it appears that the ability to infer meaning of words and phrases in context does not necessarily mean the words/phrases are actually stored in learners' memory (Mondria & Boer, 1991; Parry, 1993; Wesche & Paribakht, 1994). In other words, it does indeed take a certain intentional effort of reviewing and remembering for learners to actually store and retain the newly encountered vocabulary.

Flashcard programs might be the first tool that comes to mind when we think about vocabulary memorization. Three very commonly used flashcard building services are Quizlet (https://quizlet.com), Memrise (www.memrise.com), and Anki (https://apps.ankiweb.net). The former two are web-based and the latter is a program to install on a local device. All three services allow you to build your own decks of flashcards or use what decks that have been built and shared by others, on the computer or mobile devices. If you use a commercially published textbook, it is very likely that the companion vocabulary deck has already been built. YellowBridge also has a series of flashcards based on popular textbook series on their website (www.yellowbridge.com/chinese/flashcards.php).

Alternative to the linear word-list style that flashcard programs adopt, semantic mapping is another method that may contribute to vocabulary memorization. As "a visual strategy for vocabulary expansion and extension of knowledge by displaying in categories words related to one another" (Khoii & Sharififar, 2013, p. 202), semantic mapping involves drawing a diagram of connected words, which help learners categorize word meanings in a domain of knowledge, similar to how schemata are stored and organized in the brain. The drawing could be done on paper, with any drawing or doodling programs on the computer, or using a Web 2.0 tool such as www.bubbl.us or www.xmind.net. The advantage of the traditional pen-and-paper approach is that learners also practice writing the characters while making the map; the advantages of making it digital are the ease of making additions and alterations later on, more choices of styling, and the fact that the map does not need to be constrained to the size of the paper.

Semantic mapping may work particularly well with thematic lesson units. Figure 5.5 is an example of semantic mapping on the topic of traveling, in which the concept 旅行 [Travel] is connected to six verbs related to the planning of a trip: 订/訂 [to book]; 带/帶 [to bring]; 换/換 [to exchange]; 打 [to operate]; 买/買 [to buy]; 办/辦 [to apply], and the objects that go with each verb.

A word cloud is another tool that generates a map-like presentation of words. Instead of basing the connection on their semantic relevance, however, a word cloud applies an algorithm and presents the words according to their frequency

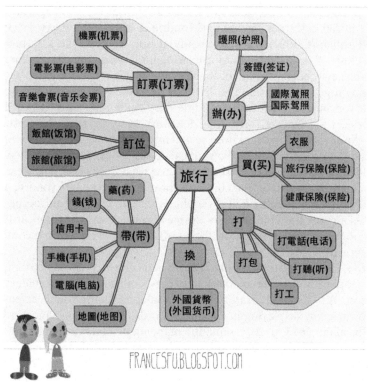

Figure 5.5 Example of semantic mapping
(Contributor: Frances Fu, Horace Mann School)

Figure 5.6 Example of word cloud of 《一件小事》 (*A Small Incident*) by 鲁迅 (Lu Xun)

of appearance and collocation in a selected text or texts. Figure 5.6 is an example of a word cloud generated from 《一件小事》 [*A Small Incident*] by 鲁迅/鲁迅 [Lu Xun] using HTML5 Word Cloud (https://timdream.org/wordcloud/).[6] However, the utilization of word clouds in new vocabulary learning is not as common as semantic mapping. It is more often used in pre-reading tasks, such as soliciting learners' prediction of the content of the reading based on the frequent key words, or character/word recognition tasks for learners to identify previously learned words and thus reinforce learning.

3. *Tools that help learners practice connecting sentences*

One challenge that many teachers face when teaching writing is that learners do have ideas and even well-formed sentences, yet they display difficulty in transitioning between them smoothly. This problem is especially prominent at the intermediate level, at which learners are developing from writing multiple loosely connected sentences to coherent paragraphs. Gaining familiarization with the rhetorical styles of Chinese writing and learning transition words (e.g., 于是/於是 [Therefore], 虽然/雖然 [although], 由于 [due to], 其次 [secondly], 总之/總之 [in summary], etc.) are the key to developing the ability to transition and produce a more coherent Chinese composition. While the best way to learn Chinese rhetoric and transition words is through actual reading (both intensively and extensively) and writing (with feedback and revision), there are some technology-enabled exercises that may help in raising awareness of these elements.

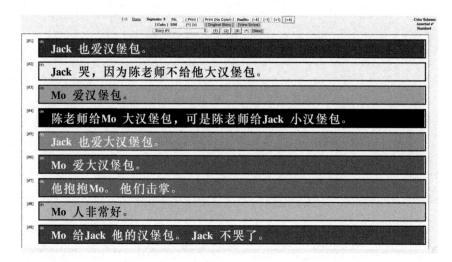

Figure 5.7 Example of paragraph scrambling using colorful stories
(Contributor: Annick Huiching Chen, Kent Denver School)

Paragraph unscrambling requires learners to put given sentences in order
to form a meaningful paragraph, which directs their attention to the transition
between ideas/sentences in the text. Two paragraph scramblers that support
Chinese are JMix exercises in Hot Potatoes (https://hotpot.uvic.ca), which is
free software that generates html pages that can be easily incorporated into
your school's LMS, and Colorful Stories exercises (see Figure 5.7) in World
Language Games (http://wlangames.net), which is a paid subscription service
that generates your own course sites and hosts your created "games" on that site.

If you are teaching novice learners, the transition between sentences might
not be an immediate concern, whereas word order *within a sentence* should
be prioritized. To this end, both Hot Potatoes and World Language Games
provide sentence unscrambling options that allow learners to put words
into a correct sentence. If you feel like generating a printed page instead of
online exercises, you may also use the Chinese Sentence and Pinyin Scramble
Creator by Arch Chinese (www.archchinese.com/chinese_sentence_scramble_
creator.html), as shown in Figure 5.8. The display can be in pinyin, Chinese
characters, or words.

4. Tools that help practice character handwriting

Whether to teach and have learners practice handwriting of Chinese characters,
especially at the beginning level, has been a major controversy among Chinese-
teaching theorists and practitioners. The stances range from viewing character
writing as a pedagogical necessity to disregarding it as a waste of time (see Shen,

Homework #1

Name: ____________________

Unscramble the Pinyin of the Chinese words or sentences using the hints provided:

1. **tā shū zhōu měi běn dú yī liǎng** (He reads about a book or two a week.)

他每周读一两本书.

2. **shàng sǎ fēi bié kā dào bǎ shū** (Don't spill coffee on the books)

别把咖啡洒到书上!

3. **yǐ kě diàn nǐ shū zhāng mǎi qù dì tú** (You can buy a map from a book store.)

你可以去书店买张地图.

4. **wǒ le dài le shū wàng** (I forgot to bring my books with me.)

我忘了带书了.

5. **wǒ xǐ shū huān zhè hěn běn** (I like this book a lot.)

我很喜欢这本书.

6. **qù shū wǒ huán qù tú guǎn le shū** (I went to the library to return books.)

我去图书馆还书去了.

Chinese Sentence Scramble Creator © 2008-2016 www.ArchChinese.com
Generated by Demo User

Page 1
Nov 19, 2016 8:30 AM

Figure 5.8 Example of print sentence unscrambling exercise using Chinese sentence and Pinyin scramble creator (Arch Chinese)

2014 for a review). Among those who choose to explicitly teach characters (both reading and writing), the timing to introduce them is another point of debate between those who advocate for immediate introduction "because the sounds, the syntax, and the characters are interrelated in a higher-level structure and they should be integrated from the first lesson" (Liu, 1983, p. 66) and those who believe in speech primacy theory (i.e., the writing system is most naturally acquired subsequent to speaking) and thus delayed introduction (see Ye, 2013 for a review). As Lam (2011) pointed out, there is no one-size-fits-all solution to character instruction. The judgment relies on the specific needs, requirements, experiences, and beliefs of each teacher in practice. Nevertheless, if you choose to have learners practice handwriting characters at any point in the curriculum, there are tools that you may utilize to make it more effective and potentially more time-efficient.

First of all, instead of demonstrating the writing of every character on your own, animated stroke order display can be found on many Chinese online dictionaries, such as YellowBridge, MDBG, and Written Chinese Dictionary. There are also programs devoted specifically to stroke order animation display, such as eStroke and Skritter, both of which have mobile app versions that are easy to use on the go. Both app versions allow learners to trace the characters and practice writing with their finger on the touch screen, and Sktitter also provides this function in their web version, as shown in Figure 5.9. You may create a teacher's account as well to track learners' use of Skritter.

Another useful technology-enhanced method for character introduction is to divide and/or highlight different character constituent components to raise awareness of the formation and reuse of common components in Chinese characters. Such effects can be achieved using common image processing tools such as PicPick or Photoshop, or using the "fragment" function in the "shape format" menu in PowerPoint (2013 or later versions) and can be used creatively for class activities. For example, in Figure 5.10, the teacher uses four consecutive slides to ask learners to identify the missing components (氵, 日, and 人) in the character 渴.

Figure 5.9 Example of character tracing practice using Skritter

Figure 5.10 Using PowerPoint slides to draw attention to character components
(Contributor: Yi Lee, Henry J. Kaiser High School)

Some teachers would like to assign character worksheets for learners to practice handwriting. For this purpose there are several online character worksheet generators to choose from, such as E-Hanzi Digital Chinese (www.ehanzi.com), eStroke (www.eon.com.hk/estroke/), and worksheet generators on Yes!Chinese (www.yes-chinese.com/tzg/) and Arch Chinese (www.archchinese.com/chinese_worksheet_maker.html).

Developing digital literacy

As mentioned in Chapter 1, digital literacy[7] is listed or embedded in most lists that aim to define the twenty-first-century skills for learners. The meaning of "literacy" and, consequently, literacy instruction, has thus been transformed to accommodate new forms of post-typographic, multimodal *text* generated with constantly evolving information and communication technologies (Leu & Kinzer, 2000; Livingstone, 2004; Jewitt, 2006; Kalantzis, Cope, & Cloonan, 2010; Lotherington & Jenson, 2011).

Alkali and Amichai-Hamburger (2004) identified five major digital skills required for digital literacy:

- Photo-visual skills: "Reading" instructions from graphical displays
- Reproduction skills: Utilizing digital reproduction to create new, meaningful materials from preexisting ones

- Branching skills: Constructing knowledge from non-linear, hypertextual navigation
- Information skills: Evaluating the quality and validity of information
- Socio-emotional skills: Understanding the "rules" that prevail in cyberspace and applying this understanding in online cyberspace communication.

To many language teachers the skills listed above may look intimidating as they seem to exceed what is traditionally considered instruction of language and literacy. However, as Kumagai, López-Sánchez, & Wu (2015) pointed out, to address the learner's need to develop multiliteracy, language learning and teaching "can no longer be solely (or mostly) concerned with language per se" and world language education needs to "move beyond current communicative and 'language-focused' approaches, and into those that prepare students to be effective producers and consumers of multimodal texts" (2015, p. xiii). While in L1 contexts these skills may be acquired across the curriculum rather than being limited to courses of language arts, in L2 contexts such acquisition, or transition of the acquired skills from L1 contexts, occurs mainly, if not solely, in the language courses. It is particularly so in foreign language classes (vis-à-vis second language classes), which describe most Chinese classes, due to the absence of a speech community in their daily life.

But how do we CFL teachers introduce digital literacy in our classes? Allen and Clementi (2016) provided a useful summary of the "knowledge processing" framework proposed by Cope and Kalantzis (coined in 2010 and elaborated in 2016) to connect literacy and language learning:

- *Experiencing*, which involves immersion in language use and communicative activities that focus on learners expressing feelings, opinions, and thoughts.
- *Conceptualizing*, which entails learners developing a metalanguage to identify and use linguistic and schematic resources that contribute to meaning making in the target language through scaffolded learning activities.
- *Analyzing*, which focuses on building learner understanding of the cultural, historical, ideological, and social contexts of texts and awareness of how the often implicit rules of language use are tied to specific contexts of communication.
- *Applying*, in which learners use new linguistic and schematic resources to reshape existing texts or create new ones.

Applying this framework in the learning of Chinese digital literacy skills, the design of learning experiences may include:

- Immersing learners with authentic Chinese digital multimodal texts (e.g., websites, forums, blogs, streamed video channels, and social media, etc.).

- Setting the course management system, course blog, wiki, or social media group (e.g., a closed group on Facebook; a Wichat Moment circle, etc.) to Chinese display to familiarize learners with the metalanguage (e.g., 关注/關注 [follow], 订阅/訂閱 [subscribe], 分享 [share], 转发/轉發 [repost], 评论/評論 [comment], 点赞/點贊 [like], 私信 [private messaging], etc.) required for independent exploration.
- Bringing learners' attention to the difference in genres and rhetorical styles between digital and traditional texts, as well as among different digital texts (e.g., the succinct writing style of Twitter or Weibo due to the character limitation, the omission of punctuation in text messaging, the hyperlinking in blog articles, and the use of emoticons, etc.).
- Discussing and analyzing diverse and sometimes conflicting perspectives in multiple sources and authors addressing the same topic. While such diversity is present in traditional texts as well (e.g., political stances of different print newspapers), the ability to assess information in an Internet environment is especially important because the content is not bound by the principles practiced by traditional press media and the sources of information have an extremely wide range of reliability.
- Having learners identify and compare *netiquette* (Internet etiquette) and cultural expectations of Chinese users (e.g., how to properly address someone in an email; what are considered appropriate causes to friend and unfriend someone on social media; whether *phubbing*[8] is acceptable in public and private social contexts, etc.)

It is also worth mentioning that the principles, activities, and tools for developing *general literacy*, as mentioned in the previous sections of this chapter, may also be used in the development of digital literacy.

In Chapter 4 and Chapter 5, we have discussed how to use technology to assist the development of oral proficiency and literacy. I cannot emphasize enough that while such technology provides us teachers tools, options, and possibilities, the needs of our learners remain of foremost importance in our design of learning experiences. In the next chapter, we are going to revisit the concept of learner-centeredness in foreign language classrooms in relation to two specific technology-enhanced approaches—digital storytelling and flipped learning.

Resources

1. Search engines for general-purpose authentic materials:
   Google: www.google.com
   Yahoo: www.yahoo.com
   Yahoo Hong Kong: https://hk.yahoo.com
   Yahoo Taiwan: https://tw.yahoo.com
   百度 (Baidu): www.baidu.com

2. Reading materials for novice/intermediate learners:
    Mandarin for Me: http://mandarinforme.com/chinese-reading-practice
    Little Fox Chinese: https://chinese.littlefox.com/en/story
    Chinese Reading Practice: http://chinesereadingpractice.com
    iChineseReaders: https://ichinesereader.com
    Learn Mandarin from Chinese Stories (web and mobile app): http://edu.
        chinese-stories.com
    Decipher Chinese (mobile app): www.decipherchinese.com
    Du Chinese (web and mobile app): www.duchinese.net
    好爸爸 (Chinese textbooks used in China): www.goodfather.com.cn/
        index.html
3. Reading materials for advanced learners:
    短美文网/短美文網: www.duanmeiwen.com
    一品故事网/一品故事網: www.07938.com
    中文阅读天地/中文閱讀天地 (The Chinese Reading World, for all
        levels): https://collections.uiowa.edu/chinese/index.html
    The Chairman's Bao (web and mobile app, for all levels): www.
        thechairmansbao.com
4. News media published in Chinese:
    人民日报/人民日報: http://paper.people.com.cn (China)
    南方周末: www.infzm.com (China)
    自由时报/自由時報: www.ltn.com.tw (Taiwan)
    苹果日报/蘋果日報: http://hk.apple.nextmedia.com (Hong Kong)
    联合早报/聯合早報: www.zaobao.com.sg (Singapore)
5. Chinese editions of global media:
    纽约时报/紐約時報: http://cn.nytimes.com
    华尔街日报/華爾街日報: http://cn.wsj.com/gb/index.asp
    BBC 中文网/BBC中文網: www.bbc.com/zhongwen/simp
    德国之声/德國之聲: www.dw.com/zh
    全球之声/全球之聲: https://zhs.globalvoices.org
6. Reading materials for specific purposes:
    Business:
    第一文库网/第一文庫網: www.wenku1.com/list/商务合同范本/
    省心范文网/省心範文網: www.shengxin118.com
    Legal:
    法律快车合同范本/法律快車合同範本: http://fanben.lawtime.cn/jishu/
    Drama:
    中国国际剧本网/中國國際劇本網: www.juben108.com
    Academic:
    论文网/論文網: www.lunwendata.com
    中国知网/中國知網: www.cnki.net
7. Chinese-English dictionaries:
    YellowBridge: www.yellowbridge.com
    MDBG: www.mdbg.net
    LINE: http://ce.linedict.com

Written Chinese (web and mobile app): www.writtenchinese.com
Pleco (mobile app): www.pleco.com

8. Chinese-Chinese dictionaries:
汉典/漢典: www.zdic.net
萌典: www.moedict.tw
百度词典/百度辭典: https://dict.baidu.com
新华字典/新華字典 (mobile app):
iOS: https://itunes.apple.com/cn/app/新华字典-商务印书馆官方正版/id1197209563?mt=8
Android: https://apkpure.com/chinese-dictionary-新华字典商务国际版/cn.dictcn.android.digitize.sw_gjxhdzd_10010
百度汉语/百度漢語 (mobile app): https://dict.baidu.com/download

9. Pop-up Chinese dictionaries (web extensions):
Zhongwen (Chrome): https://chrome.google.com/webstore/detail/zhongwen-chinese-english/kkmlkkjojmombglmlpbpapmhcaljjkde?hl=en
Zhongwen (Firefox): https://addons.mozilla.org/en-US/firefox/addon/zhongwen-chinese-english/
Perapera (Chrome and Firefox): www.perapera.org
Frill (Safari): https://frill.miknight.com

10. Object identification dictionaries (mobile apps):
Memrise (iOS): https://itunes.apple.com/us/app/memrise-language-learning/id635966718?mt=8
百度翻译/百度翻譯 [Baidu Translate]: http://fanyi.baidu.com/appdownload/download.html

Tools

1. Individual annotated reading:

Product Name	Microsoft Word
Function	Annotate documents
Difficulty Level	☆
Product Website	www.microsoft.com/en-us/store/b/word-2016

Product Name	TextEdit
Function	Annotate documents
Difficulty Level	☆
Product Website	https://support.apple.com/guide/textedit/welcome/mac

Product Name	OpenOffice
Function	Annotate documents
Difficulty Level	☆
Product Website	www.openoffice.org

Product Name	Google Docs
Function	Annotate and share documents
Difficulty Level	☆
Product Website	https://docs.google.com

2.   Cloud services:

Product Name	Google Drive
Function	Share documents and files online
Difficulty Level	☆
Product Website	www.google.com/drive/

Product Name	Dropbox
Function	Share documents and files online
Difficulty Level	☆
Product Website	www.dropbox.com

Product Name	iCloud (iOS)
Function	Share documents and files online
Difficulty Level	☆
Product Website	www.icloud.com

Product Name	OneDrive
Function	Share documents and files online
Difficulty Level	☆
Product Website	https://onedrive.live.com/

3.   Platforms for digital social reading:

Product Name	Google Docs
Function	Annotate, comment, and interact with other learners in reading tasks
Difficulty Level	☆
Product Website	https://docs.google.com

Product Name	eComma
Function	Annotate, comment, and interact with other learners in reading tasks
Difficulty Level	★
Product Website	https://ecomma.coerll.utexas.edu

Product Name	eMargin
Function	Annotate, comment, and interact with other learners in reading tasks
Difficulty Level	★
Product Website	https://emargin.bcu.ac.uk

Product Name	Classroom Salon
Function	Annotate, comment, and interact with other learners in reading and video viewing tasks
Difficulty Level	★☆
Product Website	http://srv01.pragma.cs.cmu.edu

Product Name	Hypothes.is
Function	Annotate webpages individually or as a group
Difficulty Level	☆
Product Website	https://web.hypothes.is

Product Name	zipBoard
Function	Annotate webpages individually or as a group
Difficulty Level	★☆
Product Website	https://zipboard.co

4.   Meme generators:

Product Name	Meme Generator
Function	Produce memes
Difficulty Level	☆
Product Website	https://memegenerator.net

Product Name	Rage Maker
Function	Produce memes
Difficulty Level	☆
Product Website	http://ragemaker.net

Product Name	Imgflip
Function	Produce memes
Difficulty Level	☆
Product Website	https://imgflip.com/memegenerator

Product Name	Canva
Function	Produce memes and other print media
Difficulty Level	★
Product Website	www.canva.com

5.   Comic strip makers:

Product Name	Pixon
Function	Make comic strips
Difficulty Level	★
Product Website	www.pixton.com

Product Name	Toondoo
Function	Make comic strips
Difficulty Level	★
Product Website	www.toondoo.com

Product Name	Make Beliefs Comix
Function	Make comic strips
Difficulty Level	★
Product Website	www.makebeliefscomix.com

Product Name	StoryboardThat
Function	Make comic strips
Difficulty Level	★☆
Product Website	www.storyboardthat.com

6.   Simulated media creators:

Product Name	对话泡泡产生器/對話泡泡產生器
Function	Create mock-up text messages between imaginary users
Difficulty Level	☆
Product Website	http://make.spotlights.news/bubble/

Product Name	Fakebook
Function	Create fake Facebook wall mock-ups with imaginary profiles
Difficulty Level	★
Product Website	www.classtools.net/FB/home-page

7.   E-book creators:

Product Name	Storybird
Function	Create visual storybooks with texts and illustrations
Difficulty Level	★
Product Website	https://storybird.com

Product Name	Book Creator
Function	Create visual storybooks with texts and illustrations
Difficulty Level	★
Product Website	https://bookcreator.com

Product Name	StoryBoard (Android)
Function	Transform videos into series of images (to be used as storybook illustrations)
Difficulty Level	☆
Product Website	https://play.google.com/store/apps/details?id=com.google.android.apps.photolab.storyboard

Product Name	Flipsnack
Function	Create more sophisticated and professional e-books
Difficulty Level	★☆
Product Website	www.flipsnack.com

Product Name	FlippingBook
Function	Create more sophisticated and professional e-books
Difficulty Level	★★
Product Website	https://flippingbook.com

Product Name	Joomag
Function	Create more sophisticated and professional e-books
Difficulty Level	★★
Product Website	www.joomag.com

8. Tools to add voice comments to learners' writing assignments:

Product Name	Microsoft Word
Function	Add voice comments to word documents
Difficulty Level	☆
Product Website	Use the built-in "insert voice" (Windows) or "audio notes" (Mac) functions in Word

Product Name	Voice Comments (by 121 Writing)
Function	Add voice comments to Google Docs
Difficulty Level	☆
Product Website	Accessible through "connect more apps" function in Google Drive

Product Name	Kaizena
Function	Add voice comments to Google Docs
Difficulty Level	☆
Product Website	Accessible through "get add-ons" function in Google Drive

9. Interactive whiteboards:

Product Name	Explain Everything (mobile app)
Function	Brainstorm ideas through synchronously drawing and doodling by multiple users
Difficulty Level	☆
Product Website	https://explaineverything.com

Product Name	AWW board
Function	Brainstorm ideas through synchronously drawing and doodling by multiple users
Difficulty Level	☆
Product Website	https://awwapp.com

10. Wiki sites for collaborative writing:

Product Name	Wikidot
Function	Create group-edited wiki webpages
Difficulty Level	★★
Product Website	www.wikidot.com

Product Name	PBworks
Function	Create group-edited wiki webpages
Difficulty Level	★★
Product Website	www.pbworks.com

Product Name	Mediawiki
Function	Record speech and edit audio files
Difficulty Level	★★★
Product Website	www.mediawiki.org/wiki/MediaWiki

Product Name	Google Sites (Wiki template)
Function	Create group-edited wiki webpages
Difficulty Level	★★
Product Website	https://sites.google.com/site/projectwikitemplate_en/

11. Vocabulary list generators:

Product Name	Chinese Vocab List Creator (Arch Chinese)
Function	Generate customized vocabulary lists
Difficulty Level	★
Product Website	www.archchinese.com/chinese_vocab_list_creator.html

Product Name	Vocabulary List Generator (Purple Culture)
Function	Generate customized vocabulary lists
Difficulty Level	★
Product Website	www.purpleculture.net/vocabulary-list-generator

12. Flashcard programs:

Product Name	Quizlet
Function	Make flashcards to help memorize vocabulary
Difficulty Level	★
Product Website	https://quizlet.com

Product Name	Memrise
Function	Make flashcards to help memorize vocabulary
Difficulty Level	★
Product Website	www.memrise.com

Product Name	Anki
Function	Make flashcards to help memorize vocabulary
Difficulty Level	★★
Product Website	https://apps.ankiweb.net

13. Mind mapping (semantic mapping) and word cloud tools:

Product Name	Bubbl.us
Function	Draw maps that represent the connection of words/concepts
Difficulty Level	☆
Product Website	https://bubbl.us

Product Name	XMind
Function	Draw maps that represent the connection of words/concepts
Difficulty Level	★
Product Website	www.xmind.net

Product Name	HTML5 Word Cloud
Function	Input texts to make word clouds
Difficulty Level	☆
Product Website	https://timdream.org/wordcloud/

14. Paragraph and sentence scramblers:

Product Name	Hot Potatoes (JMix)
Function	Generate paragraph scrambling exercises for learners to order sentences
Difficulty Level	★★
Product Website	https://hotpot.uvic.ca

Product Name	World Language Games (Colorful Stories)
Function	Generate paragraph scrambling exercises for learners to order sentences
Difficulty Level	★★
Product Website	http://wlangames.net

Product Name	Arch Chinese (Chinese Sentence and Pinyin Scramble Creator)
Function	Generate sentence scrambling exercises for learners to order words into sentences
Difficulty Level	☆
Product Website	www.archchinese.com/chinese_sentence_scramble_creator.html

15. Tools for character stroke tracing:

Product Name	Skritter (web and mobile app)
Function	Practice writing characters in correct stroke order
Difficulty Level	☆
Product Website	https://skritter.com

Product Name	eStroke (mobile app)
Function	Practice writing characters in correct stroke order
Difficulty Level	☆
Product Website	www.eon.com.hk/download.html

16. Character constituent fragmentation display:

Product Name	PicPick
Function	Graphic design, including character fragmentation
Difficulty Level	★★☆
Product Website	http://ngwin.com/picpick

Product Name	Photoshop
Function	Graphic design, including character fragmentation
Difficulty Level	★★★
Product Website	www.adobe.com/products/photoshop.html

Product Name	PowerPoint
Function	Design slides for presentation, including effects to make character fragmentation (using "fragment" function in "shape format" menu)
Difficulty Level	★
Product Website	www.microsoft.com/en-us/store/b/powerpoint-2016

17. Character worksheet generators:

Product Name	E-Hanzi Digital Chinese
Function	Generate character worksheets
Difficulty Level	☆
Product Website	www.ehanzi.com

Product Name	eStroke
Function	Generate character worksheets
Difficulty Level	★
Product Website	www.eon.com.hk/estroke/

Product Name	Yes! Chinese
Function	Generate character worksheets
Difficulty Level	☆
Product Website	www.yes-chinese.com/tzg/

Product Name	Arch Chinese
Function	Generate character worksheets
Difficulty Level	☆
Product Website	www.archchinese.com/chinese_worksheet_maker.html

Notes

1 Yahoo China has been closed since 2013, but Yahoo Hong Kong (https://hk.yahoo.com) and Yahoo Taiwan (https://tw.yahoo.com) remain in service. The Yahoo search engine (www.yahoo.com) also supports Chinese character input although the page itself is in English.
2 Classroom Salon may also be used to annotate videos.
3 While blogs are good tools for individual writing and peer comments, they are typically incapable of multiple authorship for one shared article entry and thus are not as effective for collaborative writing.
4 A search for online 新华字典 generates multiple returns of websites that have word lookup functions, but none of them are official sites by its publisher (Commercial Press). At the time this book was published, the only official digital version of 新华字典 is the iOS app published in June 2017.
5 As part of the debate between implicit and explicit learning, scholars differ in terms of whether such input should be accompanied by overt vocabulary instruction.
6 Although a few other word cloud tools claim to support Chinese input, their performance in segmenting words tends to be unreliable. A common problem is that they can only break the text into sentences, or series of words, but not at an actual word level.
7 Digital literacy here is broadly defined as the usage and comprehension of information in the digital age (Gilster, 1997), which may overlap and is sometimes used interchangeably with information literacy, (multi)media literacy, or multimodal literacy. It is also considered part of multiliteracies or new literacies (Kumagai, López-Sánchez, & Wu, 2015).
8 The word "phubbing" is formed by combining "phone" and "snubbing," which describes the behavior when someone is ignoring others in a social situation in favor of their phone or other mobile device.

References

Allen, H. W. & Clementi, D. (2016, October). Connecting literacy and language learning. *The Language Educator*, 22–24.

Alkali, Y. E., & Amichai-Hamburger, Y. (2004). Experiments in digital literacy. *Cyber Psychology & Behavior*, 7(4), 421–429.

American Council on the Teaching of Foreign Languages (2012). *ACTFL Proficiency Guidelines 2012*. Retrieved from www.actfl.org/publications/guidelines-and-manuals/actfl-proficiency-guidelines-2012

Arndt, V. (1993). Response to writing: Using feedback to inform the writing process. In M. N. Brock & L. Walters (Eds.), *Teaching composition around the Pacific Rim: Politics and pedagogy* (pp. 90–116). Clevedon, UK: Multilingual Matters.

Blyth, C. S. (2014). Exploring the affordances of digital social reading for L2 literacy: The case of eComma. In J. P. Guikema & L. F. Williams (Eds.), *Digital literacies in foreign and second language education*, 201.

Brown, A. L., Palincsar, A. S., & Armbruster, B. B. (1984). Instructing comprehension-fostering activities in interactive learning situations. In H. Mandl, N. L. Stein, & T. Trabasson (Eds.), *Learning and Comprehension of Text* (pp. 255–286). Hillsdale, NJ: Lawrence Erlbaum Associates.

Chang, C.-K., & Hsu, C.-K. (2011). A mobile-assisted synchronously collaborative translation-annotation system for English as a foreign language reading comprehension. *Computer Assisted Language Learning, 24*, 155–180.

Chaudron, C. (1984). The effects of feedback on students' composition revisions. *RELC Journal, 15*(2), 1–14.

Cohen, A., & Cavalcanti, M. (1990). Feedback on compositions: Teacher and student verbal reports. In. B. Kroll (Ed.), *Second language writing: Research insights for the classroom* (pp. 155–177). Cambridge, UK: Cambridge University Press.

Cope, B., & Kalantzis, M. (Eds.). (2016). *A pedagogy of multiliteracies: Learning by design.* New York: Springer.

Ede, L., & Lunsford, A. (1990). *Singular texts/plural authors: Perspectives on collaborative writing.* Carbondale, IL: Southern Illinois: University Press.

Ferris, D. R. (1995). Student reactions to teacher response in multiple-draft composition classrooms. *TESOL Quarterly, 29*(1), 33–53.

Foster, P. (1998). A classroom perspective on the negotiation of meaning. *Applied Linguistics, 19*(1), 1–23.

Gilster, P. (1997). *Digital literacy.* New York: Wiley Computer Publishing.

Gousseva-Goodwin, J. V. (2000). *Collaborative writing assignments and on-line discussions in an advanced ESL composition class.* (Unpublished doctoral dissertation, The University of Arizona, AZ.)

Hansen, J. G., & Liu, J. (2005). Guiding principles for effective peer response. *ELT Journal, 59*(1), 31–38.

Hedgcock, J., & Lefkowitz, N. (1994). Feedback on feedback: Assessing learner receptivity to teacher response in L2 composing. *Journal of Second Language Writing, 3*(2), 141–163.

Hosenfeld, C. (1977). A preliminary investigation of the reading strategies of successful and nonsuccessful second language learners. *System, 5*(2), 110–123.

Hyland, F. (1998). The impact of teacher written feedback on individual writers. *Journal of Second Language Writing, 7*(3), 255–286.

Jewitt, C. (2006). *Technology, literacy and learning: A multimodal approach.* Abingdon, UK & New York: Routledge.

Kalantzis, M., & Cope, B. (2010). The teacher as designer: Pedagogy in the new media age. *E-learning and Digital Media, 7*(3), 200–222.

Kalantzis, M., Cope, B., & Cloonan, A. (2010). A multiliteracies perspective on the new literacies. *New literacies: Multiple Perspectives on Research and Practice*, 61–87.

Keh, C. L. (1990). Feedback in the writing process: A model and methods for implementation. *ELT Journal, 44*(4), 294–304.

Khoii, R., & Sharififar, S. (2013). Memorization versus semantic mapping in L2 vocabulary acquisition. *ELT Journal, 67*(2), 199–209.

Kumagai, Y., López-Sánchez, A., & Wu, S. (Eds.). (2015). *Multiliteracies in world language education.* Abingdon, UK & New York: Routledge.

Lam, H. C. (2011). A critical analysis of the various ways of teaching Chinese characters. *Electronic Journal of Foreign Language Teaching, 8*(1), 57–70.

Lee, I. (2004). Error correction in L2 secondary writing classrooms: The case of Hong Kong. *Journal of Second Language Writing, 13*(4), 285–312.

Leki, I. (1991). The preferences of ESL students for error correction in college-level writing classes. *Foreign Language Annals, 24*(3), 203–218.

Leu, D. J., & Kinzer, C. K. (2000). The convergence of literacy instruction with networked technologies for information and communication. *Reading Research Quarterly, 35*(1), 108–127.

Li, M., & Zhu, W. (2017). Good or bad collaborative wiki writing: Exploring links between group interactions and writing products. *Journal of Second Language Writing, 35*, 38–53.

Liu, I. (1983). The learning of characters: A conceptual learning approach. *Journal of the Chinese Language Teachers Association, 18*, 65–76.

Liu, J., & Sadler, R. W. (2003). The effect and affect of peer review in electronic versus traditional modes on L2 writing. *Journal of English for Academic Purposes, 2*(3), 193–227.

Livingstone, S. (2004). Media literacy and the challenge of new information and communication technologies. *The Communication Review, 7*(1), 3–14.

Lockhart, C., & Ng, P. (1993). How useful is peer response? *Perspectives, 5*(1), 17–29.

Lotherington, H., & Jenson, J. (2011). Teaching multimodal and digital literacy in L2 settings: New literacies, new basics, new pedagogies. *Annual Review of Applied Linguistics, 31*, 226–246.

Mondria, J. A., & Boer, M. W. D. (1991). The effects of contextual richness on the guessability and the retention of words in a foreign language. *Applied Linguistics, 12*(3), 249–267.

Palincsar, A. S., & Brown, A. L. (1986). Interactive teaching to promote independent learning from text. *The Reading Teacher, 39*(8), 771–777.

Parry, K. (1993). Too many words: Learning the vocabulary of an academic subject. In T. Huckin (Ed.), *Second Language Reading and Vocabulary Learning* (pp. 109–129). Norwood, NJ: Ablex.

Paulus, T. M. (1999). The effect of peer and teacher feedback on student writing. *Journal of Second Language Writing, 8*(3), 265–289.

Penna, C., & Fallik, D. (2009). *Googles, tweets, and pods: Social media and the millennial learning,* presented at Lilly East Conference, 2009. University of Delaware.

Reid, J. M. (1993). *Teaching ESL writing.* Upper Saddle River, NJ: Prentice Hall Regents.

Reither, J. A., & Vipond, D. (1989). Writing as collaboration. *College English, 51*(8), 855–867.

Rollinson, P. (2005). Using peer feedback in the ESL writing class. *ELT Journal, 59*(1), 23–30.

Shen, H. H. (2014). Chinese L2 Literacy Debates and Beginner Reading in the United States. *The Routledge Handbook of Educational Linguistics,* 276.

Storch, N. (2002). Patterns of interaction in ESL pair work. *Language Learning, 52*, 119–158.

Storch, N. (2005). Collaborative writing: Product, process, and students' reflections. *Journal of Second Language Writing, 14*(3), 153–173.

Storch, N. (2013). *Collaborative writing in L2 classrooms.* Bristol, UK: Multilingual Matters.

Tsui, A. B., & Ng, M. (2000). Do secondary L2 writers benefit from peer comments? *Journal of Second Language Writing, 9*(2), 147–170.

Vaughn, S., Klingner, J. K., & Bryant, D. (2001). Collaborative strategic reading as a means to enhance peer-mediated instruction for reading comprehension and content-area learning. *Remedial and Special Education, 22*, 66–74.

Villamil, O. S., & De Guerrero, M. C. M. (1996). Peer revision in the L2 classroom: Social-cognitive activities, mediating strategies, and aspects of social behavior. *Journal of Second Language Writing, 5*(1), 51–75.

Villamil, O. S., & Guerrero, M. C. D. (1998). Assessing the impact of peer revision on L2 writing. *Applied Linguistics, 19*(4), 491–514.

Watanabe, Y. (2008). Peer-peer interaction between L2 learners of different proficiency levels: Their interactions and reflections. *The Canadian Modern Language Review, 64*, 605–635.

Wesche, M., & Paribakht, T. S. (1994). *Enhancing vocabulary acquisition through reading: A hierarchy of text-related exercise types.* Presented at the American Association of Applied Linguistics, Baltimore, Maryland, 1994. In ERIC Document Reproduction Service No. ED369291.

Yang, S., Zhang, J., Su, A., & Tsai, J. (2011). A collaborative multimedia annotation tool for enhancing knowledge sharing. *Interactive Learning Environments, 19*, 45–62.

Ye, L. (2013). Shall we delay teaching characters in teaching Chinese as a foreign language? *Foreign Language Annals, 46*(4), 610–627.

Zoghi, M., Mustapha, R., Maasum, T., & Mohd, N. R. (2010). Collaborative strategic reading with university EFL learners. *Journal of College Reading and Learning, 41*, 67–94.

6 Learner-centered instruction, digital storytelling, and flipped learning

As early as the late 1970s and early 1980s, scholars in second language acquisition (SLA) started advocating for learner-centered instruction in foreign language education (e.g., Papalia, 1976; Altman & James, 1981). Despite the wide recognition and promotion among scholars with theoretical and empirical support, the majority of general practice in foreign language classes remained highly teacher-centered for the next two decades (Dupin-Bryant, 2004; Liu, Qiao, & Liu, 2006). Such a discrepancy between theory and practice may be attributed to the lack of proper professional training for teachers to obtain the *know-how* of learner-centered instruction (Altman, 1983; Liu, Qiao, & Liu, 2006). As Altman (1983) pointed out, the *transformation* of one's teaching to be learner-centered relies on the understanding of the *deep structure* (beliefs and attitudes) and *surface structure* (methods and technical skills) of such an educational orientation and that "learner-centered language teachers are trained most effectively in learner-centered teacher training programs" (p. 24). Fortunately, we have witnessed an increasing number of such training opportunities since the turn of the century. Many leading centers and organizations in the field of foreign language teacher training have incorporated learner-centered instruction as one of their core values. An obvious example is the 21st Century Skills Map published by ACTFL and P21 (Partnership for 21st Century Learning, 2011). In the chart that compares the past with today's "transformed" language classroom (p. 4), not only is "learner-centered with teacher as facilitator/collaborator" (vis-à-vis "teacher-centered class") listed as a feature of today's classroom, many other listed features also reflect the nature of learner-centered instruction, such as:

- Students learn to *use* the language [emphasis added]
- Emphasis on learner as "doer" and "creator"
- Differentiating instruction to meet individual needs
- Personalized real world tasks
- Seeking opportunities for learners to use language beyond the classroom
- Learners create to "share and publish" to audiences more than just the teacher

As a consequence, more and more books, conferences, workshops, and webinars are now available about learner-centered instruction, and teachers no longer lack training opportunities, as Altman (1983) observed in the last century.

The working definition of learner-centered instruction (LCI) in this chapter is, as Kain (2003) developed, the approaches in which the construction of knowledge is shared, and learning is achieved through learners' engagement with various activities. Wang, Jensen, and Yeh (2011) put together a list of common elements of an LCI foreign language class:

- Theme-based
- Cognitively engaging real-world tasks focus on end goal
- Final performance for an authentic audience
- Authentic resources
- Teacher as facilitator
- Learner as doers
- Personalized learning
- Target language used within *and* outside of class [emphasis in original]
- Focus on all modes of communication
- Connect language learning with cultural products, practices, perspectives
- Assess all modes of communication
- Language used as a tool to support learning in other content areas

It is worth noting that all of the technologies introduced in previous chapters are already compliant with or capable of learner-centered lesson design. In this chapter, I am going to introduce two specific technology-enhanced methods that accommodate LCI particularly well: digital storytelling and flipped learning.

Digital storytelling

Digital storytelling in the field of education generally refers to the production of short personal narratives in which learners construct meaning using multiple semiotic resources enabled by media technology. The product can be seen as a "hybrid text" (Yang, 2012, p. 221) that may include voiced narratives, written texts, images, sounds, music, videos, or even interactive digital games. Studies have shown that digital storytelling benefits learners in many aspects of language learning, such as:

- Development of oral proficiency (Castaneda, 2013; Yoon, 2013; Kim, 2014)
- Enhancement of reading and writing processes (Ohler, 2006; Yoon, 2013; Sarıca & Usluel, 2016)
- Author identity construction (Nelson, 2006; Yang, 2012)
- Complex, creative, and critical thinking (Sadik, 2008; Vinogradova, Linville, & Bickel, 2011; Yoon, 2013)

- Exploration and practice of multiliteracy (Nelson & Hull, 2009; Vinogradova, Linville, & Bickel, 2011; Yang, 2012; Castaneda, 2013)
- Establishment of learner collaboration and community (Normann, 2011; Vinogradova, Linville, & Bickel, 2011; Yoon, 2013)

Learners have also responded positively to this learning experience and recognized it as engaging and motivating for self-learning as well as collaborative learning (Ware, 2008; Lotherington & Jenson, 2011; Normann, 2011; Kim, 2014; Aktas & Yurt, 2017). As Castaneda (2013, p. 55) pointed out, "students were able, willing, and proud to share personal stories in a foreign language."

Digital storytelling is in essence learner-centered because:

- It is theme-based, which creates a sense of purpose and encourages deeper inquiry into a domain of knowledge of the learner's own choice.
- The learning experience is personalized in every aspect, including choice of topic, content, narrating style, sound effects, and visual design.
- Learners are the doers while teachers are facilitators in the process of story creation.
- It is project based, with sequenced and integrated tasks that focus on the final construction of meaning.
- It connects the learning of language and other content areas.
- It may utilize authentic resources.
- It may be presented to an authentic audience.
- The process may involve all modes of communication.

Digital storytelling benefits learners the most when we see it as a long-term *process* rather than just focusing on the *product*. From brainstorming ideas to writing up initial drafts, to peer editing, to processing feedback from peers and the teacher, to revising based on these comments, and to making media-related decisions, there are ample learning opportunities for constant self-expression and meaning negotiation. Lambert's (2013) framework clearly maps out this process with seven steps towards an impactful digital story:

1. Owning your insights: By asking questions such as "what story do I want to tell" and "what it means to me," the author presents a particular lesson they learned through the story, which serves them "in negotiating their lives in the world" (p. 54).
2. Owning your emotions: The author identifies the emotions they go through in the story and conveys them to the audience with "emotional honesty" (p. 58) to help the audience understand the journey.
3. Finding the moment: It emphasizes the *moment* that things change, a dramatic highlight in the story that brings new insight or shifts in perspective.
4. Seeing your story: The author uses visuals to *bring things to life* for the audience.

5. Hearing your story: The author uses their own voice, which is the essential element that distinguishes a digital *story* from a music video or slideshow, and additional sounds and music to connect emotionally with the audience.
6. Assembling your story: This is the step where the author puts all of the visuals and audio into the story structure and make sure they work together.
7. Sharing your story: The author revisits the context of the story and verifies the match between the purpose, the content, and the intended audience, which also decides distribution scope (e.g., with a general audience online, or with a small closed group, etc.).

How do we translate such a framework into practice in a language classroom? What would we actually have learners do to incorporate these steps, leading towards the final production of a digital story? Let's look at two project timelines developed by language teachers in practice:

The first one is a 12-week project developed by Brenner (2014), in which she divided the process into three stages:

Stage 1: Pre-production

> Week 1 – Present digital storytelling project idea
> Week 2 – Introduce digital story background and show examples
> Week 3 – Software demonstration and mini-digital-story task
> Week 4 – Students begin writing narrative and selecting photos
> Week 5 – Students continue writing and selecting
> Week 6 – Students continue writing; peer editing
> Week 7 – Students complete storyboards; more peer editing

Stage 2: Production

> Week 8 – Students upload images and crop if necessary
> Weeks 9 and 10 – Students record narrative voiceovers
> Week 11 – Students fine-tune digital stories
> Week 12 – Students present digital stories

Stage 3: Postproduction

> Week 12 – Wrap-up and class feedback

The second example is a shorter, one-week project developed by Cao (2010), which involves more intensive work every day:

Monday:

1. Introduce digital storytelling
2. Research a topic

3. Write initial script (250–300 Chinese characters)

Tuesday:

1. Story circle; sharing stories
2. Create a storyboard
3. Rewrite (second draft)
4. Teacher corrects the second draft and sends it back to student

Wednesday:

1. Students practice the reading of the text
2. Record audio narration
3. Sequence images

Thursday:

1. Add music
2. Add transitions
3. Add subtitles
4. Add credits
5. Finish your final product

Friday:

1. Presentation: Students' digital stories
2. Invite your parents to come to enjoy your work

Both projects share some important components to ensure the success of the story making:

*   Both teachers introduce the concept of digital storytelling at the beginning, by presenting examples and familiarizing learners with the software. Brenner's design also had learners do a mini storytelling project to practice with the software.
*   Both projects involve peer feedback in the multi-drafting process (peer editing in the former and story circle[1] in the latter).
*   Students present their digital stories to an audience. In Cao's design, parents are also invited to this premier screening, which makes it more meaningful to the learners.

Topics of digital storytelling usually involve a personally significant moment or anecdote, but it can also be expanded to include topics of personal interest such as a historical event or a fictional work. However, as Lambert's frameworks suggest, the important factor is that a digital story is not simply created to convey *facts*, but to present *perspectives* on something meaningful to the author. Take this student's story *Red Dragonfly* (红蜻蜓) as an example, presented in Table 6.1:

Table 6.1 Digital story 《红蜻蜓》*Red Dragonfly*

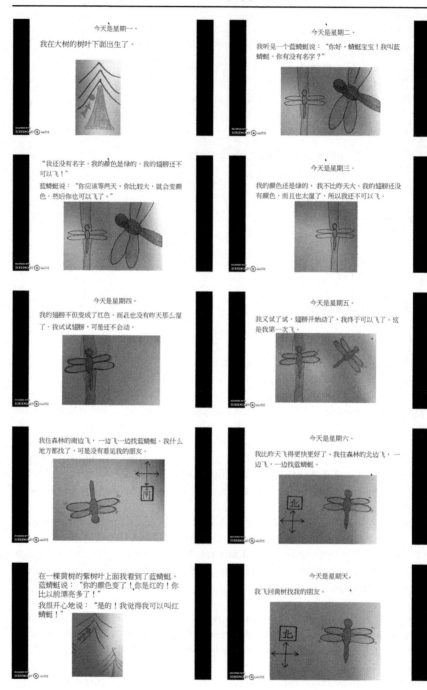

今天是星期一。

我在大树的树叶下面出生了。

今天是星期二。

我听见一个蓝蜻蜓说："你好，蜻蜓宝宝！我叫蓝蜻蜓。你有没有名字？"

"我还没有名字。我的颜色是绿的，我的翅膀还不可以飞！"

蓝蜻蜓说："你应该等两天，你比较大，就会变颜色，然后你也可以飞了。"

今天是星期三。

我的颜色还是绿的，我不比昨天大。我的翅膀还没有颜色，而且也太湿了，所以我还不可以飞。

今天是星期四。

我的翅膀不但变成了红色，而且没有昨天那么湿了。我试试翅膀，可是还不会动。

今天是星期五。

我又试了试，翅膀开始动了，我终于可以飞了。这是我第一次飞。

我往森林的南边飞，一边飞一边找蓝蜻蜓。我什么地方都找了，可是没有看见我的朋友。

今天是星期六。

我比昨天飞得更快更好了。我往森林的北边飞，一边飞，一边找蓝蜻蜓。

在一棵黄树的紫树叶上面我看到了蓝蜻蜓。蓝蜻蜓说："你的颜色变了！你是红的！你比以前漂亮多了！"

我很开心地说："是的！我觉得我可以叫红蜻蜓！"

今天是星期天。

我飞回黄树找我的朋友。

Table 6.1 (Cont.)

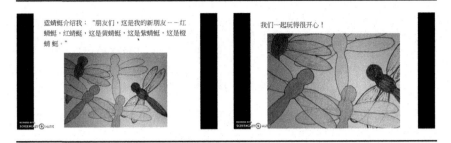

(Contributor: Julia Kim, University of Puget Sound. Instructor: Lo Sun Perry)

(Text in simplified Chinese)

今天是星期一。我在大树的树叶下面出生了。

今天是星期二。我听见一个蓝蜻蜓说:"你好,蜻蜓宝宝!我叫蓝蜻蜓,你有没有名字?"

"我还没有名字。我的颜色是绿的,我的翅膀还不可以飞。"

蓝蜻蜓说:"你应该等两天。你比较大,就会变颜色,然后你也可以飞了。"

今天是星期三。我的颜色还是绿的,我不比昨天大。我的翅膀还没有颜色,而且也太湿了,所以我还不可以飞。

今天是星期四。我的翅膀不但变成了红色,而且也没有昨天那麼湿了。我试试翅膀,可是还不会动。

今天是星期五。我又试了试,翅膀开始动了,我终於可以飞了。这是我第一次飞。

我往森林的南边飞,一边飞一边找蓝蜻蜓。我什麼地方都找了,可是没有看见我的朋友。

今天是星期六。我比昨天飞得更快更好了。我往森林的北边飞,一边飞,一边找蓝蜻蜓。

在一棵黄树的紫树叶上面我看到了蓝蜻蜓,蓝蜻蜓说:"你的颜色变了!你是红的!你比以前漂亮多了!"

我很开心地说:"是的!我觉得我可以叫红蜻蜓!"

今天是星期天。我飞回黄树找我的朋友。

蓝蜻蜓介绍我: "朋友们,这是我的新朋友--红蜻蜓。红蜻蜓,这是黄蜻蜓,这是紫蜻蜓,这是橙蜻蜓。"

我们一起玩得很开心!

(Text in traditional Chinese)

今天是星期一。我在大樹的樹葉下面出生了。

今天是星期二。我聽見一個藍蜻蜓說:"你好,蜻蜓寶寶!我叫藍蜻蜓,你有沒有名字?"

"我還沒有名字。我的顏色是綠的,我的翅膀還不可以飛。"

藍蜻蜓說:"你應該等兩天。你比較大,就會變顏色,然後你也可以飛了。"

今天是星期三。我的顏色還是綠的，我不比昨天大。我的翅膀還沒有顏色，而且也太濕了，所以我還不可以飛。

今天是星期四。我的翅膀不但變成了紅色，而且也沒有昨天那麼濕了。我試試翅膀，可是還不會動。

今天是星期五。我又試了試，翅膀開始動了，我終於可以飛了。這是我第一次飛。

我往森林的南邊飛，一邊飛一邊找藍蜻蜓。我什麼地方都找了，可是沒有看見我的朋友。

今天是星期六。我比昨天飛得更快更好了。我往森林的北邊飛，一邊飛，一邊找藍蜻蜓。

在一棵黃樹的紫樹葉上面我看到了藍蜻蜓，藍蜻蜓說：“你的顏色變了！你是紅的！你比以前漂亮多了！”

我很開心地說：“是的！我覺得我可以叫紅蜻蜓！”

今天是星期天。我飛回黃樹找我的朋友。

藍蜻蜓介紹我：“朋友們，這是我的新朋友——紅蜻蜓。紅蜻蜓，這是黃蜻蜓，這是紫蜻蜓，這是橙蜻蜓。”

我們一起玩得很開心！

(English translation)

Today was Monday. I was born under the leaves of a big tree.

Today was Tuesday. I heard a blue dragonfly say, "Hello, baby dragonfly! My name is Blue Dragonfly. Do you have a name?"

"I don't have a name yet. My color is green. My wings are not capable of flying yet." Blue Dragonfly said, "You should wait for a few days. When you get bigger, your color will change, and you can fly too."

It was Wednesday. My color was still green and I was no bigger than yesterday. My wings still had no colors and were too wet, so I still couldn't fly.

Today was Thursday. My wings not only turned red, but it was also less wet than yesterday. I tried with my wings, but could not move them yet.

Today was Friday. I tried again. My wings began to move. Finally I could fly. This was my very first time.

I flew to the south of the forest, while I was looking for Blue Dragonfly. I searched everywhere, but I could not see my friend.

Today was Saturday. I flew faster and better than yesterday. I flew to the north of the forest, looking for Blue Dragonfly.

On a purple leaf of a yellow tree I found Blue Dragonfly. Blue Dragonfly said, "Your color changed! You are red! You are much prettier than before!"

I said happily, "Yes! I think I can take Red Dragonfly as my name!"

Today was Sunday. I flew back to the yellow tree to visit my friend.

Blue Dragonfly introduced me to others, "Friends, this is my new friend—Red Dragonfly. Red Dragonfly, this is Yellow Dragonfly. This is Purple Dragonfly. This is Orange Dragonfly."

We all played together and had a great time!

Although this story did not include any reference to the learner's personal life, her central idea was very clear through the symbolic representation of the dragonfly's life. It was a story about personal growth and friendship, two themes that were significant in her life as a young adult.

This example also demonstrates that digital storytelling promotes self-learning. As a first-year learner of Chinese, the author not only maximized her use of what she had learned at that point (e.g., weekdays, colors, and sentence structures, etc.), she also searched and learned new words, phrases, and grammar in order to express meaning. What's more important is that through creating this story, she managed to express more than the sum of the individual words and patterns she had acquired in the process, which is an outcome often observed among learners telling digital stories.

For learners of higher proficiency, the content of the story may take on a research component. Take this student's story about the Qing Dynasty for example, presented in Table 6.2:

As one may see, this story included many historic facts about the Qing Dynasty, which was a result of the learner's research on this topic. However, it was still organized to support the author's point of view (i.e., the Qing Dynasty made a great contribution to the development of China), and the whole "story" reflects the author's interest (history) and is related to his personal life (his communication with his Chinese friend).

The media/tools the first student (Julia) used were hand drawings (captured by a digital camera), PowerPoint slides, and Screencast-O-Matic, a web-based screen-capturing program that also recorded her voice. The second student (Kevin) used his own photos, images obtained from the Internet, and iMovie to record his narration to each image.

There are many different tools that can be used to record a digital story. One option is to simply record your narratives directly in PowerPoint (2007 version and after for PC; 2011 and after for Mac) through its "record slide show" option in the "slide show" menu, or in Keynote (Mac) via the "audio" option in the "document" menu. It's worth noting though that currently the recorded slideshow in PowerPoint only plays within the program. When exporting the file as a movie, it loses the recorded sound. If you would like to save the story as a movie file (.mov or .mp4), you can narrate through the slideshow while operating screen-capturing tools, such as Screencast-O-Matic (web-based), ShowMore (web-based), Screencastify (Chrome browser extension), or QuickTime (Mac). These tools simultaneously record what happens on the screen and one's audio input. There are also screen-capturing apps for mobile devices: iOS devices (starting with iOS 11) have a built-in screen recording option in its control center; if your device uses the Android system, you may download independent apps such as DU Recorder or Mobizen Screen Recorder.

If you prefer more effects and video editing options, you may import images[2] into video editing programs such as iMovie (Mac), Video Remix (Windows), or Adobe Spark. Apps for tablet devices (e.g., iPad or Chromebook) that feature "interactive whiteboards" such as Explain Everything, ShowMe, and

Table 6.2 Digital story 《清朝的故事》 *Story of Qing Dynasty*

Display on screen	Voice narratives[9]
	The student talked about how he got interested in this topic: From his email correspondence with a Chinese friend he met earlier in Beijing. They share an interest in history and talk a lot about it in their emails.
	The student introduced his specific view: Although many people consider Qin the greatest dynasty of China, he personally believes Qing made an even greater contribution to the development of China.
	The student named the political, cultural, and economic contributions of the Qing Dynasty.
	The student explained how the economic expansion also unfortunately led to the Opium War and the eventual collapse of the empire.

Table 6.2 (Cont.)

Display on screen	Voice narratives[9]
	The student related the rise of the Qing Dynasty to that of current China and attributed both to their economic opening up to international trade.

(Contributor: Kevin Peters, University of Colorado at Boulder. Instructor: Fang Liang)

Educreations (iOS only) are convenient for learners to draw and doodle while recording the presentation.

Although digital storytelling is a powerful method that provides many educational benefits, there are challenges of which teachers should be aware when implementing it:

- Learners and even some teachers may be misled by the name "*digital storytelling*" and place too much emphasis on the technical components (Banaszewski, 2002; Kajder, 2004; Lambert, 2013). It is important that the teacher orients their learners at the beginning and continues reminding them that the focus of the project is to tell a good story rather than demonstrating mastery in the digital aspect.
- Not all learners are equally familiar with the concept of digital storytelling and the tools they may use to create their stories. As mentioned previously, teachers' instruction and modeling is key for learners to clearly see the value as well as the operation of such projects. Vinogradova, Linville, and Bickel (2011) also suggest that the source of expertise in regard to technology may go beyond just the instructor and include the whole *community of practice* that includes instructors, classmates, and friends, etc.
- Assessment and grading is another challenge for teachers due to the highly creative and personal nature of the project. Some teachers choose to grade learners' work based on their timely completion of each step; some place varied emphasis on language, content, and media delivery; some also look at the quality of peer editing and collaboration. Whatever your expectations are, it is important to clearly communicate them with the learners. Using a rubric to lay out expectations and revisiting it occasionally during the process could be helpful.

Flipped learning

Just as the concept of storytelling as a learning experience pre-dates digital media, flipped learning[3] also does not necessarily require utilization of modern communication technology. As defined by Bergmann and Sams (2012), flipped learning simply means "that which is traditionally done in class is now done at home, and that which is traditionally done as homework is now completed in class" (p. 13). By this definition, some teachers might have already "flipped" their classes before the digital tools became available.

However, one cannot deny that the vastly increasing attention flipped learning has attracted among teachers in the past decade is owed largely to the availability and accessibility of media production and sharing technologies that provide unprecedented convenience and freedom for teachers to create content for learners to learn at home and save the face-to-face class time for hands-on tasks and individualized projects. Nowadays, it is extremely hard to find a teacher who flips classes without utilizing technology. It is at least fair to say that technology empowers and encourages more teachers to flip their instruction. Some researchers have thus integrated the utilization of technology into the definition of flipped learning, describing it as a model of instruction "in which digital technologies are used to shift direct instruction outside of the group learning space, usually via videos." By doing so, teachers are able to "reconsider how to maximize individual face-to-face time with students" (Hamdan, McKnight, McKnight, & Arfstrom, 2013, p. 3).

A typical practice of flipped learning usually involves learners viewing a short video explaining a concept at home and then applying the concept to problem-solving tasks when they come to the next class. For instance, in a Chinese class, learners may learn expressions for comparison (e.g., 比 [more than]; 没有……那么/那麼…… [not so...as...]; 跟……(不)一样 / 一樣 [(not) same as]) via instructional videos and come to class the next day completing tasks such as comparing themselves and their peers or comparing two cities. If learners study phone manners via videos at home, they may role play different scenarios in the next class period.

Teachers who have documented the effects of flipped learning in their classes have reported predominantly positive results, including better learning outcomes, smaller gap of learners' performance, increased motivation, reduced behavioral problems, and lower learning anxiety (Papadopoulos & Roman, 2010; Bergmann & Sams, 2012; Pearson, 2012; Davies, Dean, & Ball, 2013; Baepler, Walker, & Driessen, 2014; Kim, Kim, Khera, & Getman, 2014; Yarbro, Arfstrom, McKnight, & McKnight, 2014; Huang & Hong, 2016; Hung, 2015; Ekmekci, 2017).

Flipped learning is learner-centered in its entirety because:

- It converts the content that traditionally is delivered in the format of lectures into videos or similar materials, which allows learners to have more control over and take more responsibility of their own learning.

The content is learned at a pace and in an environment in which learners are most comfortable. The constant availability of learning materials also addresses individual learners' need to revisit certain content, or to advance to the next topic without waiting until the whole class is ready to move on. Teachers may find such differentiated learning particularly effective when they are faced with a group of learners with disparate language proficiency.

- The "freed-up" class time allows for more communicative activities, hands-on projects, and collaborative learning. When learners come to class well-equipped with the linguistic or cultural knowledge learned from the video, they are more able and ready to *own* their language use in class activities. In such classrooms, the learners' role shifts from *passive listeners* to *active doers*, and the teacher's role shifts from "sage on the stage" to "guide on the side" (King, 1993, p. 1), who only provides individualized guidance and assistance when needed. Such a maximized opportunity for interaction is crucial for Category IV languages, including Chinese, as they require an average of 2200 instructional hours for learners to reach general professional proficiency.[4]

An effective flipped classroom depends on both the successful production and delivery of the video or similar material, and the design of a relevant learning experience in the classroom. Although the focus of this chapter will be on the former due to the scope of inquiry of this book, namely the utilization of technology, I would like to join the argument made by previous studies that the production and consumption of instructional videos only constitutes part of flipped learning. What is an at least equal, and arguably more important, element is how to best use the in-class time that follows (Başal, 2012; Bergmann & Sams, 2012; DeLozier & Rhodes, 2017; Ekmekci, 2017). Bloom's Taxonomy, as shown in Figure 6.1, is often referred to when scholars and experienced practitioners of flipped learning explain the relationship between the instructional videos and in-class activities.

In flipped learning the lower levels of cognitive domains in this taxonomy, namely remembering and understanding, are done through video viewing and other home assignments while the classroom activities should focus more on the higher levels of cognitive work and encourage learners to apply, analyze, evaluate, and create.

With this understanding in mind, let's steer our attention to the part that typically demands more consideration on the technological side: how to make an effective instructional video.

Bergmann and Sams (2012) laid out four steps to produce effective videos for flipped learning: planning the lesson, recording the video, editing the video, and publishing the video. Di Paolo, Wakefield, Mills, and Baker (2017) suggested a similar procedure: planning, development, delivery, and reflection. In the latter procedure, the development stage includes recording and editing, and the reflection stage is added to collect learners' feedback

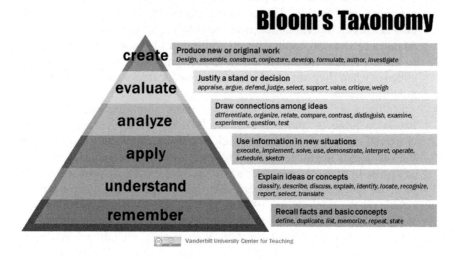

Figure 6.1 Bloom's taxonomy[7]

regarding the videos. I will combine both models and introduce the process as five stages (planning, recording, editing, delivery, and reflection) in this section. Considering teachers have widely varied skills and aptitudes for video production, I will provide separate tips for those who are considering flipped learning for the first time and have little experience with video production, and for those who have some experience flipping their classes and are ready to take on the complexity of making more sophisticated and professional instructional videos.

Table 6.3 contains four videos that can be used for flipped learning, each in different presentational styles, made with different recording/editing tools, and representing different pedagogical choices made by the teachers. I will refer to these videos as examples when discussing factors to consider and options available to teachers in each stage.

Stage 1: Planning

In this stage, teachers would first decide whether the learning content is suitable for video presentation. Given that the video assignment component of flipped learning focuses on remembering and understanding, the lower-level tasks in Bloom's Taxonomy (see Figure 6.1 above), teachers may consider the following types of content as more appropriate for video presentation:

- Content that can be made easier to understand with audiovisual demonstration

Table 6.3 Example videos for flipped learning

Topic: Introducing Others
Contributor: Fang Liang, Lantern Institute
Source: https://youtu.be/ YML1o8NPrZA
Style: Frame-in-frame lecture; acted-out scenes
Tools: Keynote, Final Cut Pro, Studio equipment

Topic: Invitation & Responding to Invitation
Contributor: Liling Huang, Boston University
Source: https://youtu.be/ yp5lKG2arq4
Style: Animation
Tools: Animaker, built-in microphone

Topic: 最近好吗? / 最近好嗎? (How have you been lately?)
Contributor: Luke Wander, the Peak School; Ye Ruan, York Prep School
Source: https://youtu.be/ U5OHOQOTxsQ
Style: Narrated slideshow; acted-out scenes
Tools: Photo Booth, iMovie, built-in webcam and microphone

Topic: 连 / 連 Structure
Contributor: Amber Navarre, Boston University
Source: https://youtu.be/ UI9y2bJKGQc
Style: Narrated slideshow; cartoon
Tools: Keynote, iMovie, Bistrips cartoon, plug-in microphone

- More complex content that may need multiple views to be fully understood or remembered
- Content that requires lengthy explanation

Some topics Chinese teachers frequently choose to flip are pronunciation rules, character formation/writing principles, common phrases, grammar explanations, and cultural presentations (e.g., origins and customs of traditional holidays). These topics may be viewed repeatedly for the purposes of learning, retention, and review. Depending on learners' proficiency level, instruction in these videos may be (partially) given in learners' first language. An additional advantage of doing such instruction via video assignment is that it reduces the use of the first language in the classroom.

After deciding that the content is suitable for video, we then need to decide how we would like the content to be presented. As seen in the example videos in Table 6.3, some teachers choose to use slides and some choose to use animations; some choose for themselves to appear on the screen and some do not; some include acted-out conversations and some focus more on concept explanation; some choose to implement a more conversational style and some choose to deliver the information more directly. The most effective way to present content depends strongly on the topic, our understanding of our learners' preferences, and our own preferences and comfort levels with different formats and tools. However, some insight about instructional video production might be borrowed from the empirical study Guo, Kim, and Rubin (2014) conducted, in which they analyzed the reaction of 128,000 learners to 862 videos on edX, one of the largest hosting sites of instructional videos. The main recommendations they made based on the findings are listed and discussed below:

- Keep the video short: learners' engagement drops significantly after 6 minutes of watching. A solution I would recommend if your topic requires explanation longer than that is to make them a series of shorter videos rather than one long video. Another convenient option is that some streaming services such as YouTube now have an editing option to divide a video into parts, and you may have your learners watch one part at a time.
- Always plan for the video format even if the lecture is recorded live. Simply recording a classroom lecture is in general NOT the best practice for instructional video production due to concerns of length, interaction style, and environmental distraction. However, if it is the most plausible way for you to make the video, try to plan ahead and keep the video production in mind when giving the live lecture, such as segmenting the lecture into sections with pauses for easier conversion into shorter video clips, rotating eye contact between the camera (your virtual students) and the students in the classroom, and if possible, testing the recording quality (both sound and image) in advance and eliminating distractions.

- Display the instructor's talking head at opportune times in the video: seeing the face of the instructor every now and then is an effective way to implement social presence in the video and thus promote learners' positive attitude and increase engagement (Richardson & Swan, 2003; Di Paolo et al., 2017).

- Strive for a one-on-one personal feel instead of high-end studio production. While a certain level of production quality is needed for content clarity, it may be encouraging for teachers to know that big-budget production does not necessarily lead to better learner engagement. Use of informal, non-studio settings may help you relate to the learners on a more personal level.

- Introduce motion and continuous visual flow (e.g., recordings of drawing or doodling) into tutorials along with extemporaneous speaking[5] for learners to follow along with the instructor's thought process. Bergmann and Sams (2012) and Di Paolo et al. (2017) disagreed on whether to use pre-written scripts during recording. I have personally tested both styles (spontaneous vs. scripted) in my own classes and found the key for success in either format depends on adapting the strengths of the alternate form. In other words, for extemporaneous instruction to succeed, the teacher must still have a coherent plan laid out despite not being completely scripted. On the other hand, for a scripted instruction to be more personal and engaging, the teacher's "performance" on the camera and/ or microphone needs to appear as natural and unrehearsed as possible.

Tips for starters: It would be easier to start making your first video by modifying your existent lesson slides rather than creating something completely from scratch. When making modification to the slides, consider two things:

1. Adjust them to appropriate lengths. Remember the ideal length of the video is 6 minutes or shorter. If you are explaining something complicated, consider breaking it into a series of shorter videos.

2. Add highlights. In a face-to-face classroom, we may easily bring learners' attention to a specific part of the text or image on the screen by pointing at it, with our hand or a laser pointer, or even by simply looking at it while learners follow our gaze. In a recorded slideshow, however, highlights have to be added differently by using colors, shapes (e.g., circling the key words), lines, or effects (e.g., flashing). If you prefer a more controlled presentation, you may create the highlights in your slide creation program (e.g., PowerPoint, Keynote, or Google Slides); if you want it to be more spontaneous, several apps allow you to doodle while you record the screencast. Since this latter method happens during recording, the tools will be introduced in Stage 2: Recording.

Tips for mastery: Once you have gained initial experience, comfort, and confidence in making instructional videos, you might want to consider expanding your content presentation methods that make the learning experience even more effective and enjoyable but require more advanced recording/editing techniques. Such options may include but are not limited to: embedding the teacher's talking head in your explanation slides, as in the first example listed above (Introducing Others), adding acted-out dialogues to demonstrate contextualized language use (e.g., Introducing Others; 最近好吗? /最近好嗎? [How have you been lately?], using animation (e.g., Invitation & Responding to Invitation), and including self-assessment exercises in the video (e.g., 连/連 Structure). Tools for these purposes will be introduced in Stage 2: Recording.

Stage 2: Recording

As stressed earlier, teachers may plan to present the content in different ways in the videos they make depending on various factors. Some topics are better presented in certain ways. For instance, when teaching different ways to invite someone out, including acted-out scenes would be highly effective. On the other hand, a lesson on Chinese word order might be best presented in the form of a narrated slideshow while displaying the text in the slides with highlights. The teacher's choice of presentation methods and styles may impact the tools they choose to use for recording and editing, which we will discuss in the current and the next sections.

In this section, I will introduce four types of recording that teachers may choose from: 1) narrated slideshow, 2) teacher's talking head, 3) acted-out scenes, and 4) animation. Please note that although each recording method involves using a unique set of tools and techniques, the recorded content may be combined in the editing stage. An example is the video "Introducing Others" in Table 6.3, which joins a narrated slideshow with an embedded teacher's talking head and inserted acted-out scenes.

1. Recording a narrated slideshow

The aforementioned recording tools for digital stories also work for teachers to record narrated slideshows, including direct recording in PowerPoint or Keynote (Mac) and using screen-capturing tools such as Screencast-O-Matic (web-based), Screencastify (Chrome browser extension), or QuickTime (Mac). Some teachers prefer to export slides as images and record their narration slide by slide in video editing programs such as iMovie (Mac), Video Remix (Windows), or Adobe Spark. An advantage of recording this way is that if you make a mistake in your speech, you do not need to redo the whole recording. You may just re-record the single slide where the mistake occurred. If you feel like changing some of the content in the video later, you may also do it easily by recording the part you want to change, instead of re-recording the whole presentation. Some teachers also use a combination of screen-capturing and editing programs to harness the convenience of the former and the flexibility of the latter. If they make any mistake during their narration, they just say it again in the correct form without stopping the recording, and simply trim the mistake part out later using an editing program.

For universal viewing experience, I would recommend that the slideshow be saved or exported as .mov or .mp4 files, which can be played on most media players and accepted by most streaming services if you plan to share the video as a link rather than as a whole file—we will discuss more about sharing options in the "delivery" stage later.

Another element to consider when making a video in the format of narrated slideshow is whether to use doodling for highlights during recording. Basic doodling can be easily done in PowerPoint with its "pen" option during presentation (accessible through the menu on the bottom left corner on the slide, or by pressing ctrl+p), as shown in Figure 6.2. In Keynote this function is currently only available on an iPad, on which you can hold your finger on the screen to bring up a color pen menu. Screen-capturing tools also tend to have the option of using a "pointer" curser that can be used to highlight a certain area on the screen, as shown in Figure 6.3.

If you are looking for more advanced drawing options, apps for tablet devices that feature "interactive whiteboards" such as Explain Everything, ShowMe, and Educreations (iOS only) allow you to draw easily with your fingers on the touchscreen while recording the presentation.

Figure 6.2 Example of doodling on a slide using PowerPoint

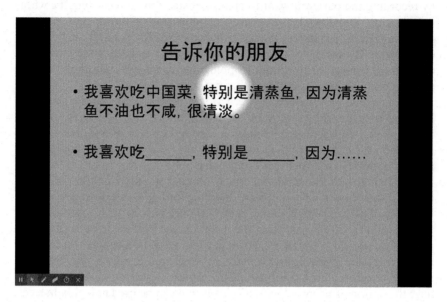

Figure 6.3 Example of using a pointer cursor during recording (Screencastify)

2. Recording the teacher's talking head

As discussed above, seeing the teacher's talking head at opportune times in the video may have a positive affective impact on learners and further motivate learning. If you choose to take advantage of this effect, there are two options: record it as an embedded window simultaneously with the screen presentation or record it as its own track and edit it into the video via post-production. The former is easy to set up and can conveniently have the whole video recorded in one sitting and the latter gives the teacher more control over when and how their talking head appears on the screen.

> **Tips for starters:** Although showing the teacher's face has a positive affective impact on learners, it does not mean you must include it in your video. As mentioned in the previous stage, you may ease into flipped learning by simply converting your existing lesson slides into a narrated slideshow. When you feel more comfortable about recording yourself, I recommend you start with the method of recording your face and the presentation screen simultaneously because it is technically easier and requires less editing effort.

If you choose to record your talking head simultaneously with a slide presentation, the aforementioned screen-capturing tools (e.g., Screencast-O-Matic,

Figure 6.4 Recording embedded talking head during presentation (QuickTime)

Screencastify, and QuickTime) all have the option of recording the screen (your slides) and the webcam (your face) simultaneously. Screencast-O-Matic and Screencastify (Chrome only) have the option when you set up your preferences at the beginning of each recording. In QuickTime (Mac) you will have to do it as two steps: first start "new screen recording" in the "File" menu to record the screen, and then start "new movie recording" to record your face with the webcam. Since the second action brings up a camera display of your face on the screen (which you can enlarge or shrink to any size you like), the first screen recording will actually have both the slide presentation and the webcam recording on it, as shown in Figure 6.4.

Some teachers may feel like having more control over the display of their talking head in the video. For instance, even if you are comfortable with being on camera, you might not want to be on the screen *all the time* throughout the video. Or, for demonstrating the pronunciation of a specific word, you could enlarge your face display temporarily and then resume the normal side-screen setting. If you would like such flexibility, you may consider filming your talking head speech as separate tracks and then insert them into any part of the video, at any preferred size or position on the screen. "Introducing Others" in Table 6.3 is a great example of utilizing this method, rotating between displays of only the teacher's talking head, only the slide show, and a combination of both on the screen. Please note that doing so does require more advanced editing techniques, which we will discuss in Stage 3: Editing.

You may use your webcam on the computer, camera on a mobile device, or a camcorder to record this part of your presentation. Mac users can use Photobooth, iMovie, or QuickTime to record webcam videos, and Windows users can use the Camera app or Video Remix. Camtasia is another option for both Mac and Windows that can do both screen and webcam recording, as well as editing. Smart phones and tablet computers nowadays tend to have video recording options in their photo apps. Using these built-in functions generates no additional cost, but if you have a little money to invest in your video projects, I would recommend getting a plug-in microphone rather than using the built-in ones for better sound recording quality. If you plan to use mobile devices or a hand-held camcorder to record most of the time, also consider buying a tripod to hold the device to maximize visual stability.

Another factor to consider when filming human figures is lighting. Avoid excessive brightness as it is distracting. Conversely, too little lighting damages the visual clarity and impedes comprehension. For an easy and inexpensive arrangement of lighting, you may use several desk lamps and experiment with them to find the best layout.

Once you have your camera, microphone, and lighting equipment ready, remember to do several test recordings and make fine adjustments (e.g., how close you should be to the camera; where you should place the microphone; whether to add or lose some lighting, etc.) for best results.

> **Tips for mastery:** If you are up for bringing your video production to a professional level, you may consider filming your videos in a studio setting, with a professional camera, lighting, and sound proofing. Recording in a studio maximizes visual and sound quality, but it could be very costly and requires a professional team to operate. I would recommend talking to the IT department or language centers of your school first to see what support you may acquire from them. You might be surprised to find out that such services are actually available in your work environment.

3. Recording acted-out scenes

As seen in the example videos "Introducing Others" and "最近好吗/最近好嗎？" ("How have you been lately?"), acted-out dialogues help demonstrate appropriate language use in context. Simply displaying text of the dialogue on the screen may be convenient as it does not require any extra recording effort, but it fails to immerse the learners in the situated interaction.

The tools mentioned above for filming the teacher's talking head may also be used to record acted-out scenes. However, when recording scenes with multiple speakers, it is especially important to adjust the camera, lighting, and microphone(s) so that the images and voices of all actors are clear to the audience.

To situate a dialogue in context, you may either record the scene in a place where the dialogue may possibly occur, as in the example of "最近好吗/

Figure 6.5 Example of green-screen effect[8]

最近好嗎?" ("How have you been lately?"), or use a "green screen" effect, as in the example of "Introducing Others." As shown in Figure 6.5, a green-screen effect typically involves using a solid-color screen, usually green or blue, as the background during recording and then key in a background image in its place during postproduction. This effect is particularly useful when the context of the dialogue is somewhere less accessible, such as an airport, or a historical site in China.

To take advantage of the green screen effect, one needs to invest in a solid-color screen and learn the required editing techniques to replace it with the preferred background during editing. I would suggest that you first consult the IT department or language center in your institution to see what support they may provide. If you are to do it on your own, see the discussion in Stage 3: Editing for more information.

4. Recording with animations

An alternative to using human actors for dialogues is to create the scene with animation, as seen in the example video "Invitation & Responding to Invitation." While it does not completely simulate a real-life scene, it does provide a more contextualized learning experience than just text and the teacher's lecture. An advantage of using animation is that it requires fewer resources (e.g., time and space for scene shoots, available human actors, effort in editing, etc.). As mentioned in Chapter 4, animation tools may be web-based, such as Go!Animate, Powtoon, Nawmal, and Animaker, or mobile apps, such as Sock Puppets and Toontastic.

Stage 3: Editing

The amount and level of editing needed for your video varies depending on how you planned and recorded your video. For instance, narrated slideshows require a minimum amount of editing, while inserted scenes with green-screen effects require more editing. However, even for the most simplistic videos, aiming to do absolutely no editing may be very challenging, simply because it is natural to make mistakes when we talk, such as a false start to mispronunciations, or forgetting to click for a certain text/effect to show up on the slide as you go. Whereas in a live classroom self-correction seems normal and does not interrupt the flow of instruction, it is more salient and thus more distracting in a video context. Although a small number of errors and quick recoveries may make the lecture more conversational and relatable, having an excessive number would probably damage the quality of instruction. An easy way to reduce errors in the video without having to re-record the whole lecture from the start is to do some simple editing to take out the parts where errors occur. During recording, if you say something wrong in a sentence, simply repeat the sentence correctly and move on. Having some pause between the incorrect and correct sentences helps you to find where to trim more easily later. After you are done recording the whole presentation, you may trim the sentences that contain the errors.

Tips for starters: If you are new to video editing, I suggest you keep editing to a minimum: trimming out the unwanted parts. If you are comfortable with trying some basic techniques, you can consider joining multiple clips (useful when you want to insert acted-out scenes) and adding transitions between them.

If you choose to upload your videos to YouTube, it provides a very easy interface to trim your video (Edit > Enhancement > Trim). If you want to trim the video file on your local machine, trimming is one of the basic functions provided in all video editing programs, such as iMovie (Mac only), Filmora, Camtasia, Shotcut, and Adobe Premiere.[6]

Programs designed specifically for video editing work more or less similarly. They tend to have a "timeline" for you to add, trim, and join clips, a preview window for you to see your edits, and command menus for you to conduct editing of the video. Here are the basic functions you may want to explore in the program:

- Importing and adding clips
- Trimming
- Voice recording (if you choose to record to imported images directly in the program)
- Adding music and effects
- Adding transition
- Adding subtitles

While it is not possible to introduce in detail how to perform all these editing functions in every available editing program, I list below their official webpages that include step-by-step user guides and/or tutorial videos for your reference:

iMovie: http://help.apple.com/imovie/mac
Filmora: https://filmora.wondershare.net/filmora-101/
Camtasia: www.techsmith.com/tutorial-camtasia.html
Shotcut: https://shotcut.org/tutorials/
Adobe Premiere: https://helpx.adobe.com/premiere-pro/tutorials.html

Once you are familiar and comfortable with the editing process, you may consider exploring:

- Chroma keying, which is the function that replaces the green screen backdrop with your preferred background image.
- Picture-in-picture (PIP) video overlay, which can be used to merge two videos (or one video and one image) into one, as demonstrated in Figure 6.6.

PIP is the technique that allows us to embed the teacher's talking head during screen presentation (e.g., Screencast-O-Matic; Screencastify). But if you decide to record the teacher's speech separately and then merge it with other visual media (slides, images, or another video clip), PIP overlay is the effect you would look for in the editing program.

Although PIP videos often have one visual display as a smaller "window," as shown in Figure 6.6, it is not the only way to use this function. For instance, in the first example "Introducing Others," this function was used in combination with green screening to have the teacher talk in the front and the blackboard-style slideshow display in the back. The two displays were seamlessly merged into one rather than having distinct boundaries between them.

This function can also combine more than two displays, as shown in Figure 6.7, in which the instructor asks learners to compare the language use between two embedded scenes. Although this function may take extra time to learn through product or user tutorials, it could be a powerful tool for teachers who want to bring their videos up to another level of creativity.

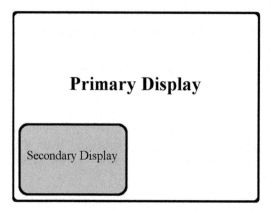

Figure 6.6 Illustration of frame-in-frame display

Figure 6.7 A PIP video with multiple embedded frames

Tips for mastery: Advanced editing options such as chroma keying and picture-in-picture video overlay tend not to be included in the basic "editing 101" style tutorials. In order to find useful guides you need to do a specific key word search to bring up relevant results. It could be done on the support forum of a specific product, or simply through

Google or YouTube searches. If you choose to do the latter, please make sure you include 1) the specific effect you are looking for, 2) name of the program, and 3) your operating system. Here is an example: "chroma keying Camtasia Mac," which brings up several very detailed step-by-step video tutorials on a Google search. You may add the version of your program (e.g., Camtasia Studio 9) and/or the generation of your operation system (e.g., Windows 10) to further narrow it down if necessary.

Stage 4: Delivery

After the editing stage, the video is made and ready to be published. The next question to consider is then where and in what format we want it to be shared and accessed? Do we share it as a file for learners to download to their personal device, or do we share it on a video stream service, such as YouTube or Vimeo, that requires an Internet connection to view? Do we share it with the general public, or do we limit access to our own classes?

There is no right or wrong answer to those questions and we must choose based on what makes the most sense to us and to our learners. For instance, the advantage of sharing the video as a downloadable file is that learners do not need to have a constant Internet connection to view it, while the advantage of sharing it on a streaming service is that it can be accessed conveniently anywhere and on multiple devices as long as there is an Internet connection. Sometimes it is not even an either-or question, because many streaming services also provide the option to allow viewer downloads. On the other hand, if you choose to share your videos as downloadable files on a learning management system (LMS, e.g., Blackboard, Moodle, or Canvas), learners can still access the video anywhere there is an Internet connection. In fact, many LMS nowadays also have built-in media players that allow learners to watch the video without actually downloading it.

Another important factor to consider is the potential reach of your video. Streaming services usually allow users to choose to share their videos either to the public or as "unlisted" videos, which means the videos do not show on a public video list and cannot be found using the search function on the streaming site, or via a search engine. Instead, you have to share the link to the specific video with learners for them to view it. However, you must keep in mind that this method still allows *anyone* with the link access so if your learners share the link with other people, they will also be able to view your video. Theoretically, the only way to limit the access of a video to a designated group of people is to share it in a restricted-access environment, such as a Google folder shared with your students, a closed Facebook group, or on an LMS as a non-downloadable video. However, even in such environments the access is restricted only in a relative sense. If someone *really* wants to show your video to others, there are always means to do so, such as screen capturing, or even simply recording it using a camera outside of the display device.

I am stressing the point that there is no way to ensure that your videos will always only be accessible to a limited population because I want to bring your attention to the copyright issue. If you use any music, images, video clips, or any material that is not created by yourself, make sure you comply with copyright law by using it the way it is licensed or obtain permission from the original author. One convenient function to use when you search images on Google is to specify usage rights under "advanced search" in the "settings" menu. Set the filter to images that are free to use, share, or modify, depending on how you want to use it. Visit the page where the image is hosted (i.e., do not simply drag and download from the preview on Google) and download from there. Often times the webpage includes information about how to properly credit the work. An example is Figure 6.5, which I used above to demonstrate green-screen effect. I found it via an advanced search on Google Images, clicked on the image, and it took me to its original page on Flickr, where I found out about the author and license information that I then listed in the endnote.

Many video-making applications also have a collection of media materials you are licensed to use in your productions, as long as you own the program legally. For instance, iMovie (Mac) has a good number of sounds, including many jingles, available for use; Adobe Spark has a gallery of images and themes for users to choose from; Video Remix (Windows) have a collection of interactive 3D objects that users may customize and incorporate in their video stories.

You may also choose to publish your video with embedded exercises for learners to self-assess their learning. It can be done during recording, with questions asked in the video and answers revealed after a pause, as seen in the video example "连/連 Structure." It can be done during editing as well. Camtasia, for instance, has a built-in video quiz/survey function that allows the teacher to embed questions into the video. It can also be done after the video is uploaded to a steaming service. As mentioned in Chapter 4, there are applications (e.g., Edpuzzle and PlayPosit) that allow users to insert interactive content, including questions to be responded to, into a streamed video.

Stage 5: Reflection

Di Paolo et al. (2017) included this stage to make instructional video production a cycle rather than ending at the publication of an individual video. The insight collected from evaluating and reflecting on the effect of one video may be applied to the next to make improvements.

There are two main questions we can ask ourselves and our learners in this stage: 1) Does the video successfully perform the instructional purpose? 2) Does it have a positive affective impact on the learners and motivate them for further learning?

To gather insight for the first question, we may conduct a comprehension check when the class regroups after the video assignment, as Bergmann and Sams (2012) suggested. The goal of this comprehension check is to verify learning and identify questions or gaps of knowledge that need further explanation, clarification, or modeling. In-class comprehension checks can be done via simple tasks (e.g., a short role-play conversation), Q&A between the teacher and students, interactive games or poll responses, etc. A controversial method to check comprehension after watching the video is quizzes. Although quizzes may help motivate learners to watch the videos (Enfield, 2013), the grading side of it might not be justifiable because as I stressed earlier, watching the instructional video as a home assignment is only half of the flipped learning experience. It is useful to conduct a formative assessment for the purpose of checking learners' progress at this point, yet doing the assessment for grading purposes might not be ideal because the learning experience is not complete until the in-class half is also practiced, which is designed for learners to reach true mastery of the learned concept through hands-on activities and projects.

There are other ways to motivate learners to watch the videos than giving a graded quiz. For instance, teachers may also have learners complete worksheets or take notes while watching the video and collect them in the next class meeting. The written record may provide us with more data about individual learners' intake of the content. In addition, having learners do some tasks while watching promotes active learning and helps learners to keep their minds, not just their eyes, on the video lesson. If you share a video with embedded questions made by interactive tools (e.g., Camtasia, Edpuzzle, or PlayPosit), they also allow you to track learners' progress based on their responses to the questions.

Although having learners complete tasks during or after viewing may encourage them to watch the assigned content, the most important factors for learners to watch instructional videos regularly might instead be affective, which include learners' mental readiness and perception of flipped learning (Hao, 2016) and whether they consider the videos attractive (Enfield, 2013). Therefore, it is important to find out how learners *feel* about the videos after watching them.

Teachers may already incorporate elements that make their videos more relatable and enjoyable to the learners, such as bringing in drama (e.g., Examples "Introducing Others," "Invitation & Responding to Invitation," and "最近好吗/最近好嗎？" ["How have you been lately?"]) or using humor (e.g., "最近好吗/最近好嗎？" ["How have you been lately?"] and "连/連 Structure"), but whether learners actually like to watch the videos and respond positively to this method of learning may not be revealed until you actually collect feedback from them.

A questionnaire survey may be very helpful to get to know what learners like or dislike about your videos in general. If teachers intend to solicit more specific feedback about individual videos, they may include a comment section on the worksheet they give learners to complete at home.

Making one's own flipped videos may be very challenging at the beginning until you get used to the practice, and even after that, making high-quality videos is always time-consuming and effort-intensive. One suggestion I would like to make, which hopefully would be encouraging to teachers who are considering flipping their classes, is that you do not have to make every video on your own. When I started flipping my classes in 2010, there were not many good instructional videos available in Chinese so I ended up making hundreds of videos on my own. Since more and more Chinese teachers have flipped their classes and made videos for this purpose, we can now first search the Internet to see if someone has already shared videos of the topics we would like to flip.

If you do not find a video that works for you and decide to make one for your learners, you still do not need to do it completely on your own. You can collaborate and divide work with your colleagues, or even reach out to teachers outside of your school and work with them. Workshops on flipped learning are a good place to meet teachers who have shared interests. Online networks and forums on this topic might also land you a potential collaboration.

One more thing to keep in mind is that you do not have to flip all of your class content, and for the content you do choose to flip, it does not always need to be in the form of videos. Videos are powerful media and all of the flipped classroom teachers I have worked with and interviewed use videos, but we do not have to use videos *all the time*. For instance, I flip my classes both with videos and with reading materials that prepare them for in-class activities. The latter is done through digital social reading, which we discussed in Chapter 5.

Tools

1.   Slideshow technologies:

Product Name	PowerPoint
Function	Create and present slides with option of recorded narration
Difficulty Level	★★
Product Website	https://products.office.com/powerpoint

Product Name	Keynote
Function	Create and present slides with option of recorded narration
Difficulty Level	★★
Product Website	www.apple.com/keynote/

Product Name	Google Slides
Function	Create and present slides with option of recorded narration
Difficulty Level	★★
Product Website	www.google.com/slides/about/

2.   Screen-capturing tools:

Product Name	Screencast-O-Matic
Function	Capture screen activities and audio input on the computer
Difficulty Level	☆
Product Website	https://screencast-o-matic.com

Product Name	Screencastify
Function	Capture screen activities and audio input on the computer
Difficulty Level	☆
Product Website	www.screencastify.com

Product Name	ShowMore
Function	Capture screen activities and audio input on the computer
Difficulty Level	★
Product Website	https://showmore.com

Product Name	QuickTime (Mac)
Function	Capture screen activities and audio input on the computer
Difficulty Level	★
Product Website	https://support.apple.com/downloads/quicktime

Product Name	Screen Recording (iOS)
Function	Capture screen activities and audio input on a mobile device
Difficulty Level	☆
Product Website	Accessible from iOS device's Control Center

Product Name	DU Recorder (Android)
Function	Capture screen activities and audio input on a mobile device
Difficulty Level	☆
Product Website	https://play.google.com/store/apps/details?id=com.duapps. recorder

Product Name	Mobizen Screen Recorder
Function	Capture screen activities and audio input on a mobile device
Difficulty Level	☆
Product Website	https://play.google.com/store/apps/details?id=com.rsupport. mvagent

3. Video recording and editing tools:

Product Name	iMovie (Mac)
Function	Record and edit videos
Difficulty Level	Basic recording: ★
	Advanced editing: ★★☆
Product Website	www.apple.com/imovie/

Product Name	Camtasia
Function	Record and edit videos
Difficulty Level	Basic recording: ★
	Advanced editing: ★★★
Product Website	www.techsmith.com/video-editor.html

Product Name	Shotcut
Function	Edit videos
Difficulty Level	★☆
Product Website	www.shotcut.org

Product Name	Filmora
Function	Edit videos
Difficulty Level	★☆
Product Website	https://filmora.wondershare.net/filmora-video-editor.html

Product Name	Adobe Premiere
Function	Record and edit videos
Difficulty Level	Basic recording: ★
	Advanced editing: ★★★
Product Website	www.adobe.com/products/premiere.html

Product Name	Video Remix (Windows)
Function	Record and edit videos, photos, and 3-D animations
Difficulty Level	★☆
Product Website	Accessible via Microsoft "Photos" app
	https://support.microsoft.com/en-us/help/17205/
	windows-10-create-videos

Product Name	Adobe Spark
Function	Record and edit videos, photos, and webpages
Difficulty Level	★☆
Product Website	https://spark.adobe.com/

Product Name	Photobooth (Mac)
Function	Take photos and videos with computer camera
Difficulty Level	☆
Product Website	https://support.apple.com/guide/photo-booth/

Product Name	Camera (Windows)
Function	Take photos and videos with computer camera
Difficulty Level	☆
Product Website	www.microsoft.com/en-us/store/p/windows-camera/9wzdncrfjbbg

4.   Interactive whiteboard apps with recording function:

Product Name	Explain Everything
Function	Create multimedia narratives with interactive whiteboard
Difficulty Level	★
Product Website	https://explaineverything.com

Product Name	ShowMe
Function	Create multimedia narratives with interactive whiteboard
Difficulty Level	★
Product Website	www.showme.com

Product Name	Educreations (iOS)
Function	Create multimedia narratives with interactive whiteboard
Difficulty Level	★
Product Website	www.educreations.com

5.   Animation tools:

Product Name	GoAnimate
Function	Make animated videos with cartoon characters
Difficulty Level	★★
Product Website	https://goanimate.com/

Product Name	Powtoon
Function	Make animated videos with cartoon characters
Difficulty Level	★★
Product Website	www.powtoon.com/

Product Name	Nawmal
Function	Make animated videos with cartoon characters
Difficulty Level	★★
Product Website	www.nawmal.com

Product Name	Animaker
Function	Make animated videos with cartoon characters
Difficulty Level	★★
Product Website	www.animaker.com

Product Name	Sock Puppets (iOS mobile app)
Function	Make animated videos with sock puppet characters
Difficulty Level	☆
Product Website	https://itunes.apple.com/us/app/sock-puppets/ id394504903?mt=8

Product Name	Toontastic (iOS and Android mobile app)
Function	Make animated videos with cartoon characters
Difficulty Level	★
Product Website	https://toontastic.withgoogle.com

6. Tools for embedding interactive content in videos

Product Name	Edpuzzle
Function	Embed interactive content into a video
Difficulty Level	★
Product Website	https://edpuzzle.com/

Product Name	Playposit
Function	Embed interactive content into a video
Difficulty Level	★
Product Website	www.playposit.com

Product Name	Camtasia
Function	Edit videos (including embedding interactive content)
Difficulty Level	Basic recording: ★ Advanced editing: ★★★
Product Website	www.techsmith.com/video-editor.html

Notes

1 A story circle is where storytellers presents their developing story ideas in a small group and receive feedback from each other.
2 If you would prefer to import slides created in PowerPoint or Keynote into video editing programs, you need to first export the slides "as images" and then import them.
3 "Flipped learning" has also been called "flipped class(room)", "flipped teaching", or "inverted/reverse instruction."
4 The full list of languages in each category and their required contact hours for professional mastery are available at: www.state.gov/m/fsi/sls/c78549.htm.
5 The authors referred to such a style of presentation as Khan-style tutorials, as it is commonly used in the instructional videos of the Khan Academy, one of the earliest non-profit online services featuring tutorial videos for educational purposes.
6 Movie Maker (Windows) used to be a popular video editing program as well. It was discontinued by Microsoft in 2017 and the company has yet to release a successor to it. They released Video Remix (within the Photo app) in 2017 as one video editing option. However, it does not provide the full features a typical video editing program does (e.g., picture-in-picture frames).
7 This graphic was created by the Center for Teaching, Vanderbilt University and was downloaded from www.flickr.com/photos/vandycft/29428436431. License link: https://creativecommons.org/licenses/by/2.0/legalcode
8 This graphic was created by Category5 TV and was downloaded from www.flickr.com/photos/category5tv/6508366751. License link: https://creativecommons.org/licenses/by/2.0/
9 Since this is a much longer video, I summarized the student's narrative (originally in Chinese) to highlight his organization and the progression of ideas.

References

Aktas, E., & Yurt, S. U. (2017). Effects of digital story on academic achievement, learning motivation and retention among university students. *International Journal of Higher Education, 6*(1), 180–196.

Altman, H. B. (1983). Training foreign language teachers for learner-centered instruction: Deep structures, surface structures and transformations. *Georgetown University Round Table on Languages and Linguistics, 83*, 19–26.

Altman, H. B., & James, C. V. (1981). Foreign language teaching: Meeting individual needs. *World Englishes, 1*(1), 64–70.

Baepler, P., Walker, J., & Driessen, M. (2014). It's not about seat time: Blending, flipping, and efficiency in active learning classrooms. *Computers & Education, 78*, 227–236.

Banaszewski, T. (2002). Digital storytelling finds its place in the classroom. *Multimedia Schools, 9*(1), 32–35.

Başal, A. (2012). The use of flipped classroom in foreign language teaching. *The 3rd Black Sea ELT Conference Proceedings*, 8–12. Samsun, Turkey (November 2012).

Bergmann, J., & Sams, A. (2012). *Flip your classroom: Reach every student in every class every day*. Washington, DC: International Society for Technology in Education.

Brenner, K. (2014). Digital stories: A 21st-century communication tool for the English language classroom. *English Teaching Forum*, *52*(1), 22–29.

Cao, H. (2010, May). *Digital chinese storytelling*. Presented at CLTA-GNY 2010 Annual Conference, New York.

Castaneda, M. E. (2013). "I am proud that I did it and it's a piece of me": Digital storytelling in the foreign language classroom. *CALICO Journal*, *30*(1), 44–62.

Davies, R. S., Dean, D. L., & Ball, N. (2013). Flipping the classroom and instructional technology integration in a college-level information systems spreadsheet course. *Educational Technology Research and Development*, *61*(4), 563–580.

DeLozier, S. J., & Rhodes, M. G. (2017). Flipped classrooms: A review of key ideas and recommendations for practice. *Educational Psychology Review*, *29*(1), 141–151.

Di Paolo, T., Wakefield, J. S., Mills, L. A., & Baker, L. (2017). Lights, camera, action: Facilitating the design and production of effective instructional videos. *TechTrends*, *61*(5), 452–460.

Dupin-Bryant, P. A. (2004). Teaching styles of interactive television instructors: A descriptive study. *The American Journal of Distance Education*, *18*(1), 39–50.

Enfield, J. (2013). Looking at the impact of the flipped classroom model of instruction on undergraduate multimedia students at CSUN. *TechTrends: Linking Research and Practice to Improve Learning*, *57*(6), 14–27.

Ekmekci, E. (2017). The flipped writing classroom in Turkish EFL context: A comparative study on a new model. *Turkish Online Journal of Distance Education*, *18*(2), 151–167.

Guo, P. J., Kim, J., & Rubin, R. (2014, March). How video production affects student engagement: An empirical study of mooc videos. In *Proceedings of the first ACM conference on Learning at scale (L@S) conference* (pp. 41–50). ACM.

Hamdan, N., McKnight, P., McKnight, K., & Arfstrom, K. M. (2013). The flipped learning model: A white paper based on the literature review titled "A review of flipped learning." Retrieved from https://flippedlearning.org/wp-content/uploads/2016/07/WhitePaper_FlippedLearning.pdf

Hao, Y. (2016). Middle school students' flipped learning readiness in foreign language classrooms: Exploring its relationship with personal characteristics and individual circumstances. *Computers in Human Behavior*, *59*, 295–303.

Huang, Y. N., & Hong, Z. R. (2016). The effects of a flipped English classroom intervention on students' information and communication technology and English reading comprehension. *Educational Technology Research and Development*, *64*(2), 175–193.

Hung, H. T. (2015) Flipping the classroom for English language learners to foster active learning, *Computer Assisted Language Learning*, *28*(1), 81–96.

Kajder, S. B. (2004). Enter here: Personal narrative and digital storytelling. *English Journal*, *93*(3), 64–68.

Kain, D. J. (2003). Teacher-centered versus student-centered: Balancing constraint and theory in the composition classroom. *Pedagogy*, *3*(1), 104–108.

Kim, M. K., Kim, S. M., Khera, O., & Getman, J. (2014). The experience of three flipped classrooms in an urban university: An exploration of design principles. *The Internet and Higher Education*, *22*, 37–50.

Kim, S. (2014). Developing autonomous learning for oral proficiency using digital storytelling. *Language Learning & Technology*, *18*(2), 20–35.

King, A. (1993). From sage on the stage to guide on the side. *College Teaching*, *41*(1), 30–35.

Lambert, J. (2006). *Digital storytelling: Capturing lives, creating community* (2nd ed.). Berkeley, CA: Digital Diner Press.

Lambert, J. (2013). *Digital storytelling: Capturing lives, creating community* (3rd ed.). Abingdon, UK & New York: Routledge.

Liu, R., Qiao, X., & Liu, Y. (2006). A paradigm shift of learner-centered teaching style: Reality or illusion. *Arizona Working papers in SLAT, 13*, 77–91.

Lotherington, H., & Jenson, J. (2011). Teaching multimodal and digital literacy in L2 settings: New literacies, new basics, new pedagogies. *Annual Review of Applied Linguistics, 31*, 226–246.

Nelson, M. E. (2006). Mode, meaning, and synaesthesia in multimedia L2 writing. *Language Learning and Technology, 10*(2), 56–76.

Nelson, M. E., & Hull, G. A. (2008). Self-presentation through multimedia: A Bakhtinian perspective on digital storytelling. In K. Lundby (Ed.), *Digital storytelling, mediatized stories: Self-representations in new media* (pp. 123–144). Bern, Switzerland: Peter Lang Publishing.

Normann, A. (2011). *Digital storytelling in second language learning: A qualitative study on students' reflections on potentials for learning* (Master's thesis, Norwegian University of Science and Technology, Department of Social Sciences and Technology Management, Program for Teacher Education).

Ohler, J. (2006). The world of digital storytelling. *Educational Leadership, 63*(4), 44–47.

Papadopoulos, C., & Roman, A. S. (2010). *Implementing an inverted classroom model in engineering statistics: Initial results.* American Society for Engineering statistics. Proceedings of the 40th ASEE/IEEE Frontiers in Education Conference, Washington, DC.

Papalia, A. (1976). *Learner-centered language teaching: Methods and materials* (Innovations in foreign language education). Rowley, MA: Newbury House.

Partnership for 21st Century Learning (2011). *21st century skills map: World languages.* Retrieved from www.p21.org/storage/documents/Skills%20Map/p21_worldlanguagesmap.pdf

Pearson, G. (2012). Biology teacher's flipped classroom: 'A simple thing, but it's so powerful'. *Education Canada, 52*(5), web exclusive. Retrieved from www.cea-ace.ca/education-canada/article/biology-teacher's-flipped-classroom-'-simple-thing-it's-so-powerful

Richardson, J. C., & Swan, K. P. (2003). An examination of social presence in online courses in relation to students' perceived learning and satisfaction. *Journal of Asynchronous Learning, 7*(1), 68–88.

Sadik, A. (2008). Digital storytelling: A meaningful technology-integrated approach for engaged student learning. *Educational Technology Research and Development, 56*(4), 487–506.

Sarıca, H. Ç., & Usluel, Y. K. (2016). The effect of digital storytelling on visual memory and writing skills. *Computers & Education, 94*, 298–309.

Vinogradova, P., Linville, H. A., & Bickel, B. (2011). "Listen to my story and you will know me": Digital stories as student-centered collaborative projects. *TESOL Journal, 2*(2), 173–202.

Wang, S., Jensen, J., & Yeh, M. (2011, November). *How to facilitate learner-centered language learning and teaching.* Presented at ACTFL Annual Conference, Denver, Colorado.

Ware, P. (2008). Language learners and multimedia literacy in and after school. *Pedagogies: An International Journal, 3*(1), 37–51.

Yarbro, J., Arfstrom, K. M., McKnight, K., & McKnight, P. (2014). *Extension of a review of flipped learning.* Retrieved from https://flippedlearning.org/wp-content/uploads/2016/07/Extension-of-FLipped-Learning-LIt-Review-June-2014.pdf

Yang, Y. F. D. (2012). Multimodal composing in digital storytelling. *Computers and Composition, 29*(3), 221–238.

Yoon, T. (2013). Are you digitized? Ways to provide motivation for ELLs using digital storytelling. *International Journal of Research Studies in Educational Technology, 2*(1), 1–10.

7 More tools, teacher resources, and peace of mind

In this last chapter I am going to introduce more technological tools in light of current trends and emerging developments on the horizon. These tools might not be as directly related to language instruction as the technologies introduced in the previous chapters but could still contribute to creating more effective and enjoyable learning experiences. I will include technologies in the following categories:

1. Learning management
2. Game-based learning and gamification of learning
3. Teacher sharing and collaboration

At the end of this chapter, I will also invite my reader-teachers to think about the prospect of their future technology use, and how to keep peace of mind while facing overwhelmingly rapid changes and developments in the field of instructional technology.

Technologies for learning management

Although a broader definition of learning management may include the whole design of the learning experience, in this discussion I will only focus on the tools and services that help teachers conduct administrative and logistical management, such as sharing learning materials, tracking learners' progress, distributing and collecting assignments, and classroom management. These functions are not directly related to the learning tasks but nevertheless serve as an integral component of successful operation of a learning environment.

To many of us, learning management systems (LMS, also known as Course Management Systems), as the name suggests, come to mind first when considering tools for learning management. Some commonly used LMSs include Blackboard, D2L, Moodle, Canvas, Edmodo, Schoology, Absorb, and Google Classroom. All LMSs are able to perform the core functions of learning management, such as material sharing, learning module creation, discussion forum hosting, giving quizzes and assignments, and keeping grades. Since most schools already have their school-wide LMS installed and it is not up to the individual teachers to choose one for their own courses, I will not include a detailed comparison of these systems. Such comparisons are available from other sources. For instance, *PC Magazine* just published an article, "The best (LMS) Learning Management Systems for 2018" (Fenton, 2018). In less common cases where the LMS is not provided to the teacher by the institution, one may want to explore free open source options (e.g., Moodle, CourseSites,[1] Canvas, Schoology, or Google Classroom) rather than industrial models that tend to be costly.

Most schools provide training to their teaching faculty in regard to how to use their chosen LMS. I would strongly recommend teachers attend the training and also talk to the IT support at your school to find out about the "hidden functions" that are not always mentioned in the general training but may be useful specifically for language courses. For instance, Blackboard allows teachers to annotate learners' assignment via "grade assignment," including direct drawing on the document, which could be useful for correcting character writing; Canvas allows learners to directly record a video and even add captions in their assignments. If there is anything you wonder if your LMS can do, asking the IT department of your school would be the quickest way to find out, and an alternative would be searching the LMS's product website, which often has a forum for you to post your questions.

LMSs are not the only services that help teachers to collect and organize learners' work. Given that the assignment types allowed in LMSs are not specifically designed for language learners, many teachers seek more interactive alternatives for their home assignments. I have introduced many tools that could collect learners' language performance samples in different modes in Chapter 4 and 5, to develop learners' oral proficiency and literacy. In this section, I would like to mention several additional tools that focus on more micro-level language exercises:

1. Liveworksheets.com (web-based)

This platform allows teachers to create their own interactive "worksheets" for learners to complete online. The exercise types include multiple choice (click and choose), text answers (typing), matching (draw lines; drag and drop objects), and voice recording. Teachers may also browse worksheets created and shared by other teachers. Figure 7.1 is an example of results produced by searching "Chinese" exercises on this site.

2. Tinytap (mobile app)

Tinytap provides similar functions to Liveworksheets.com, but its flipbook[2] style allows learners to journey through pages and its colorful themes (accessible via its "creation packs" in "create") are particularly enticing for younger learners. Figure 7.2 and 7.3 illustrate what an activity on Tinytap may look like (Contributor: Moses Sia, Pauseability): In this flipbook titled

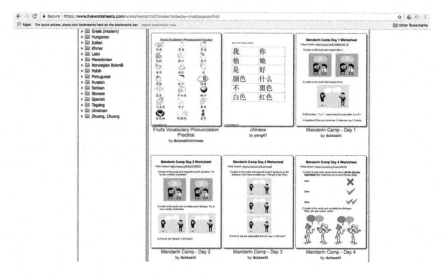

Figure 7.1 Public exercises on Liveworksheets.com

穿哪件衣服呢？(Which Clothes to Wear?), learners start with a page that shows a rabbit and two shirts (Figure 7.2). They hear a pre-recorded question, "请你帮我选一件衬衫，谢谢。/ 請你幫我選一件襯衫，謝謝。(Please help me pick a shirt. Thank you.)" When they tap and choose one of the two shirts, they hear the corresponding phrase 长袖衬衫/長袖襯衫 (long sleeve shirt) or 短袖衬衫/短袖襯衫 (short sleeve shirt) and see its meaning on the screen. They go on to choose pants and socks for the rabbit on the next pages. At the end of the book (Figure 7.3), the rabbit wears the exact options the learner has chosen for it and thanks them.

It is worth noting that although Tinytap activities may be played by learners either in its mobile device apps (both Android and iOS) and computers in web browsers, creation of new activities currently can only be done within their mobile apps.

3.   Classkick.com (Chrome browser only)

Although both Liveworksheets.com and Tinytap allow teachers to track learners' progress by using their "my students" (Liveworksheet.com) or "classes" (Tinytap) functions, they feature immediate and automated feedback rather than the teacher's comments or peer collaboration.[3] If you are seeking these sophisticated functions, you may consider Classkick.com. Classkick.com adopts a slide-by-slide journey style, similar to Tinytap, and allows learners to type, draw, voice-record, and upload images or links to answer questions (see Figure 7.4). It has two icons, "please help" and "please

Figure 7.2 Example of Tinytap activity (first page)

Figure 7.3 Example of Tinytap activity (last page)

check," for learners to seek help while working on the assignment. The teacher may also choose to turn on "student helpers" so that learners may help in answering questions and checking the work of their peers.

Learning management also includes classroom management, which involves tools and techniques that help keep learners attentive and on task

Figure 7.4 Teacher-learner interaction on Classkick.com
(Contributor: Je-Yu Chu, Pacific Academy)

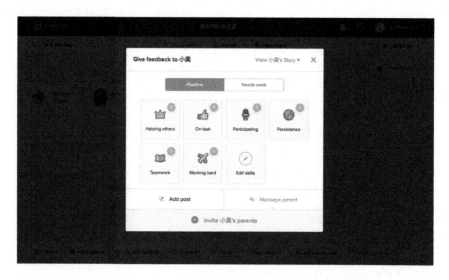

Figure 7.5 Point-awarding system for learners' classroom behavior (ClassDojo)

in the classroom. ClassDojo (www.classdojo.com) and Class123 (https://
class123.ac) are two of the most popular classroom management services,
both featuring 1) a point system for tracking and awarding learners' positive
classroom behavior (see Figure 7.5 for example), 2) a learner portfolio builder,
which allows learners to take pictures/videos of their work, 3) a teacher-parent

communication system, in which the teacher can share learners' performance records with the parents, and they can message one another without using their own phone number, and 4) a handy set of tools such as group maker, random student generator, and timer, etc.

Game-based learning and gamification of learning

More and more educational games and/or game-like elements have been integrated in instructional designs in twenty-first-century classrooms, as practitioners and scholars recognize the gains of learning effects, social skills, and motivation among learners (Buckingham, 2014; New Media Consortium, 2014; Flores, 2015). In this section, I will focus on the technologies and related techniques due to the scope of inquiry of this book. If you feel like learning more about the relation between gaming and education, or gaming and second language learning in particular, please see Kapp (2012) and Flores (2015), respectively, for more information.

I will make a distinction between game-based learning and gamification of learning experiences, as the tools for each purpose differ. The former refers to adoption of games for educational purposes (Caponetto, Earp, & Ott, 2014), while the latter involves an overall incorporation of game design into a non-game context (Werbach & Hunter, 2012), in this case, the language course. In other words, playing a word puzzle game in a class would be considered game-based learning, while using an awarding system for learners to earn points/badges by completing learning quests laid out through the whole curriculum would be considered gamification of the learning context. I will introduce technologies for each purpose in the discussion below.

1. Technologies for game-based learning

The types of games that can be adopted for the purpose of language learning are virtually indefinite, as long as they align with the learning objectives and instructional design. One may not even need to use gaming-specific tools to create such games. For instance, using Exit Effects (in the "Animation" menu) on objects in PowerPoint would allow teachers to create click-and-reveal games for learners to identify (Figure 7.6), match (Figure 7.7), or guess (Figure 7.8). In order to trigger the exit effect when clicking on each object (e.g., rectangle shapes), use the Trigger in the Animation Pane to map the effect to each object (currently only available on Windows). If you wish for the revealed part to be covered again, check the "Rewind when done playing" box in the "Timing" window.

Combining animation effects and hyperlinks to different slides allows teachers to create quiz games in the format of jeopardy. Luckily, Microsoft already have templates created for such games (for both Mac and Windows), available on their official site under the category of "Education" (https://templates.office.com/en-us/Education).

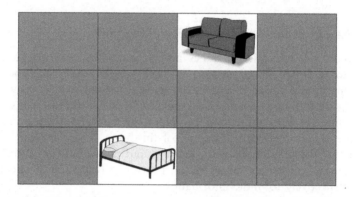

Figure 7.6 Object-identification game using PowerPoint

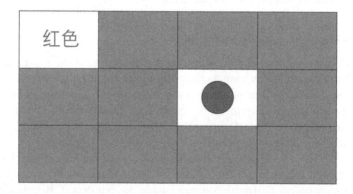

Figure 7.7 Matching game using PowerPoint

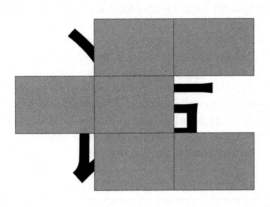

Figure 7.8 Guessing characters using PowerPoint

Many teachers also like to use Kahoot, Quizizz, or Quizlet Live for more engaging quiz games; each has their own appealing characteristics. In general, Kahoot (https://kahoot.com/) features a highly exciting gameplay as learners' reaction time is part of the game. In other words, learners need to be both accurate and fast to win the game. After answering each question by clicking the option on their mobile devices or computers, a scoreboard is projected on the screen to show top players' names,[4] which further incentivizes the competition. Many learners find the expectation for quick reaction in Kahoot fun and exciting, yet it may cause certain a certain level of performance anxiety for some learners. If your learners tend not to appreciate such intensity, you may instead set up Kahoot "Challenges"[5] (accessible via the "My Kahoots" menu). Challenges allow learners to go through the game in a more individualized context as long as they complete it before a set deadline. Although each question is still timed and the high scores on the scoreboard still go to those who respond both quickly and accurately, the competition is not in front of the whole class and may thus reduce performance anxiety.

If you seek to completely remove the time factor, Quizizz (https://quizizz.com) may be a suitable platform for your games. Questions and answer options in Quizizz are displayed on learners' own devices rather than on the shared projected screen, and the gameplay is completely self-paced. Learners may take as much time as they need for each question without their ranking on the leaderboard being penalized.

If not all of your learners have a device to play these digital games, you may consider playing Kahoot in Team Mode, an option on the screen after you click on the "Play" button on the "My Kahoot" menu. Or, alternatively you may choose Quizlet Live. Quizlet Live is one mode available on Quizlet (https://quizlet.com/), which was introduced in Chapter 5 as a flashcard service to help learners memorize vocabulary. Once you have a set of flashcards, you may click on the set and choose "Live," which will automatically generate quiz games for learners to participate in. Unlike Kahoot and Quizizz, which may be played by individual learners, Quizlet Live is designed to be played by teams and encourages collaboration. Each team will play on one shared device and compete against other teams. Quizlet Live also gives teachers the flexibility to either randomize or customize team members. Since the games are designed to be played by teams, you need at least four learners in order to play Quizlet Live.

In addition to the games introduced above that require the teacher's design, there are also commercially developed games, many of which are mobile apps, that are ready out of the box. While these games are typically designed for self-learning and might not be appropriate as a whole-class activity, they might come in handy on a few occasions:

- Due to the issue of enrollment or educational resources (e.g., classrooms or budget), some teachers are faced with the challenge of teaching mixed-level learners as one group. Self-learning materials, including games, help the teacher to perform differentiated instruction. For instance, the teacher may focus on helping more advanced learners with a presentation while assigning learners with lower proficiency to play a self-paced language game, or vice versa. Most self-learning games have varied levels of difficulty for learners to choose from.
- Depending on the area, it could be difficult to find qualified substitute teachers for some of us. Self-learning games provide alternative lesson plans for substitute teachers who do not even know Chinese to execute.
- Because learners tend to love these games, some teachers use them as awards (e.g., 5-minute play time) to encourage positive classroom behaviors (e.g., staying in the target language; finishing a task early; helping classmates, etc.).

Duolingo, a popular app for learning different languages just officially released its Chinese course in 2017. The "course" offers content up to A2 level of CEFR and level 3 of HSK,[6] and adopts many game elements, such as avatars, points, leveling up, and achievement badges. The app focuses more on receptive skills such as sound recognition and form/meaning identification (see Figure 7.9) rather than productive skills such as speaking and writing.

Microsoft Learning Chinese is another mobile app (iOS) that provides a game-like learning experience. The "Learn" option leads the learner through phrases and sentence structures with simple English explanations; the "Speak"

Figure 7.9 Example exercise in Duolingo

option adopts the voice-typing technology introduced earlier and provides graded feedback (see Figure 7.10). However, as pointed out in Chapter 4, such technology does not perform well in discerning different tones and thus the grading does not provide reliable feedback to this end.

If you are looking for a Chinese game app that is designed specifically for younger learners, you may look into Fun Chinese. Targeting age 3–10, Fun Chinese features colorful cartoon scenes and easy-to-operate fingertip games. However, the content is more limited (~100 words) compared to Duolingo and Microsoft Learning Chinese.

Word Swing Chinese is another game app that plays quite differently from the ones introduced above. It is a text adventure game for learners of intermediate or higher proficiency. The text adventures are interactive non-linear stories that give readers choices at different points in the story. Based on the reader's choices, the story unfolds differently (see Figure 7.11).

2. Gamification of learning

As mentioned earlier, gamification of learning refers to the conversion of the whole learning context into a game-like system, which typically involves

Figure 7.10 Example speaking exercise in Microsoft Learning Chinese
(Image used with permission from Microsoft)

integrating consistent gaming elements through the whole curriculum. In a gamified learning context, learning tasks are considered *quests*; upon completion of each quest, learners receive *points*; points often lead to certain *awards*, which could be realistic (e.g., gifts or extra credits) or symbolic (e.g., in-game titles, trophies, or badges). The two classroom management systems introduced above, ClassDojo and Class123, are great examples of such integration.

In a more sophisticated game system, points are also cumulated for learners to *level up*. Once they reach a higher level, they can challenge themselves with more difficult and complicated quests, which in turn grant more points to the learners. Teachers may also design bigger projects or summative assessment to be *bosses* in this game world. Successful completion of boss-level challenges tends to give learners a tremendous sense of achievement, even beyond the awards themselves.

To cultivate a sense of learning/gaming community, one may allow learners to collaborate and compete as *teams*. The teacher may also choose to implement *leaderboards* that show top-performing players. Although leaderboards tend to be exciting and motivating in games, I would recommend that teachers

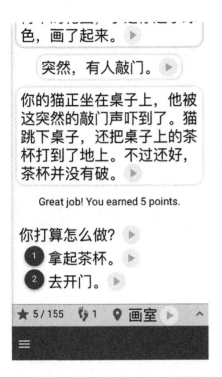

色，画了起来。

突然，有人敲门。

你的猫正坐在桌子上，他被这突然的敲门声吓到了。猫跳下桌子，还把桌子上的茶杯打到了地上。不过还好，茶杯并没有破。

Great job! You earned 5 points.

你打算怎么做？
1 拿起茶杯。
2 去开门。

★ 5 / 155 🐾 1 📍 画室

Figure 7.11 Text adventure game (Word Swing Chinese)

use them with caution. In order to make the learning/gaming experience more fun and inclusive, you will want to award a bigger variety of achievements. In addition to academic "performances," teachers can be creative and award things like "best acting in role plays," "most hilarious stories," "most time invested in self-learning materials," "asking great questions," or "making/eating the most dumplings," just to name a few.

ClassDojo and Class123 are not the only gamified learning management platforms. Academy (www.growthengineering.co.uk/academy-lms/) is an LMS with a clean and intuitive design for course gamification. An e-learning specialist once described it as "not an LMS that has gamification added, it's an LMS that relies on gamification to function at all" (Ingwersen, 2018). It encompasses all the features of gamification noted above and can be customized based on the teacher and learners' needs. However, it could be a costly option without budgetary support from the school.

Edmodo (www.edmodo.com) is a more cost-effective option that provides a basic system for the teacher to award badges. Its Facebook-like interface also encourages learners to post, comment, and see the status of their collected badges if they choose to share. In addition to the gamifying features, Edmodo may serve as a platform that allows learners to experience social media in a

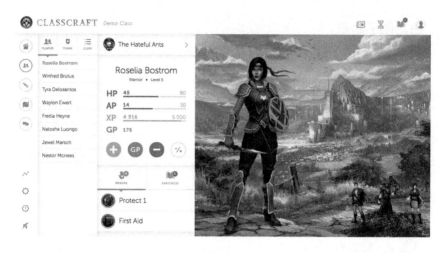

Figure 7.12 Class system for Heroes in Classcraft

more controlled/monitored environment. As mentioned in Chapter 5, development of digital literacy includes preparing our learners socio-emotionally with the (often unspoken) expectations and interpretive frameworks of online communication. Using a social media platform with the teacher's mediation may provide a valuable opportunity to engage learners in such discussion.

If you are a hardcore gamer yourself and crave an ultimate gaming system that captures the spirit of an archetypical fantasy RPG (role-playing game), you may consider Classcraft (www.classcraft.com). If you are not familiar with such games, on the other hand, I would recommend that you choose something more simplistic from the options I have mentioned above.

The basic/free subscription of Classcraft allows learners to choose a *class* for their hero from three options: warriors, mages, or healers,[7] each with their own powers and skills. Figure 7.12 shows a warrior's stats as an example. In the game, learners may earn XP to level up, lose and gain HP to stay alive in the game, spend AP to use their hero's abilities, spend GP to buy new outfits, and use PP to learn new hero powers. Points are earned during the campaign through learning quests, and/or from the teacher's manual awarding for positive behaviors. Learners collaborate in teams to conquer the quests and may use their powers to help one another. Figure 7.13 demonstrates the scoreboard of teams showing their current points. As mentioned earlier, establishing a reasonable balance between types of awardable achievements is very important for cultivating a positive learning/gaming atmosphere. In Classcraft, since learners may take HP damage for negative behaviors, it is particularly important for the teacher to be mindful with their awarding of points so that the overall experience is fulfilling rather than punitive.

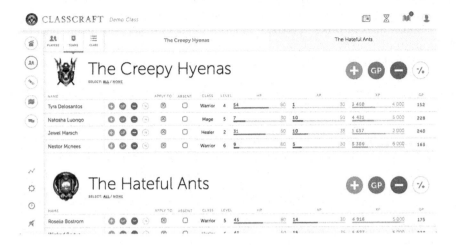

Figure 7.13 Scoreboard of teams in Classcraft

Teacher sharing and collaboration

Thanks to the advancement of modern communication technology, sharing and collaboration among Chinese teachers has been compounded. With the Internet, social media, and virtual communication services, you may learn from master teachers all over the world, have your questions answered, obtain materials others have developed, share your own brilliant ideas about teaching with others, and participate in collaborative projects, even if you are the only Chinese teacher in your institute. Three major types of sharing/collaboration will be discussed in this section: 1) Sharing through personal venues, 2) online teacher communities, and 3) collaborative projects.

1. Sharing through personal venues

Many Chinese teachers use blogs, personal websites, individual accounts on social media, or stream video channels to reflect on their teaching experiences and share their ideas or materials with the public. As a matter of fact, many examples I have used in this book came from these venues. For instance, the example of animated video in Chapter 4 came from Practical Chinese (https://communicateinchinese.com), a website developed by Liling Huang on Chinese pragmatics; the example of semantic mapping in Chapter 5 came from Learn Chinese Teach Chinese (http://francesfu.blogspot.com), a blog on Chinese learning and teaching by Frances Fu; the example of dismantling character components in PowerPoint in Chapter 5 came from Yi Lee's Mandarin Teaching Center (www.facebook.com/AlohaMandarin/), a Facebook page developed by Yi Lee. I do not personally know most of these teachers, but this book, as well as many Chinese teachers in the field, benefits from their generous sharing of teaching-related insights and resources.

Some blogs or other "personal" sharing venues are actually maintained by a group of teachers, such as Ignite Language (http://tprsforchinese.blogspot. com), a blog featuring teachers' reflections on learning activities, particularly in TPRS classrooms, by four cross-language teachers. I solicited the example of movie talk in Chapter 3 from one of their authors, Diane Neubauer. I still categorize such group-maintained sharing channels as personal venues rather than teacher communities, which I will introduce in the next section, because the sharing in such venues is mostly unidirectional. Viewers may interact with the authors by leaving comments or contacting them via messaging if allowed by the setting, yet only the author(s) may publish the main materials (e.g., posts on blogs or videos on streaming channels) and do the majority of sharing.

2. Online teacher communities

As I just mentioned, the main difference between personal sharing venues and teacher communities is that in the latter, authorship is less limited and tends to be executed in a self-volunteered manner. Social media groups and discussion forums are two major types of such communities, in which every member may post and respond as they wish.

Where one joins such online communities often depends on the social platforms they prefer to use. For instance, I am personally a Facebook user and the groups I have joined include: CLTA 中文电影兴趣小组/中文電影興趣小組, 国际汉语教师—线上备课社团/國際漢語教師—線上備課社團, 中文教学百宝箱/中文教學百寶箱, K-12 Chinese Teachers' Discussion Group, and Mandarin Chinese Teachers in the UK, etc. My colleague uses WeChat more often than Facebook, so she is a member of: 国际汉语教师500强/國際漢語教師500強, 继承语教学工作室/繼承語教學工作室, 跨学科汉语教学/跨學科漢語教學, etc.

Most topic-based groups and/or discussions on social media (e.g., Facebook, Reddit, or Twitter) can be found via a keyword search on the service if you wish to join them, with an exception of WeChat. In order to find and join a group on WeChat, one needs to be invited by a member of the group, or somehow have access to the group's QR code. It is also worth mentioning that personal venues hosted on these social media sites can also be found via a keyword search, such as "pages" on Facebook or "public accounts" on WeChat.

3. Collaborative projects

Connections over the Internet may lead to collaborative projects among teachers. Before modern communication technology, such collaboration could only be achieved among teachers of the same or nearby schools; nowadays, teachers are able to communicate and work together using online collaborative tools regardless of where they are or whether they have even met in person.

For instance, "Do as the Chinese Do" is an on-going project that produces animated videos introducing Chinese words and idioms. The continuous publication of their materials relies heavily on recruitment of volunteers (e.g., Chinese teachers, voice-actors, and production technicians) from their WeChat account and Facebook page (www.facebook.com/DoAsChineseDo/). 慢速中文/Slow Chinese (www.slow-chinese.com), a website that publishes podcasts on news and cultural topics on a weekly basis, is another non-profit project that is led by a group of enthusiastic Chinese teachers and volunteers.

Yanjun Liu, who is a member of 慢速中文/Slow Chinese, also led two other long-distance collaborations among Chinese teachers and published 《真实语料学中文/真實語料學中文/*Authentic   Materials   for   Chinese Teaching and Learning*》 (Liu, 2016. Downloadable at: www.teach-chinese. com/download/) and 《短片里的中国/短片裡的中國/*Understanding China through Video Clips*》 (Liu, 2018. Downloadable at www.teach-chinese.com/ download/), mentioned in Chapter 3 and 5, respectively. Each collection resulted from a joint effort of tens of voluntary Chinese teachers from all over the world.

Collaboration among teachers is not limited to material creation and compilation. For instance, the aforementioned Facebook group, 国际汉语教师—线上备课社团/國際漢語教師—線上備課社團 (www.facebook.com/groups/ huayuL2/), has several subgroups in it, one of which is called 国际笔友夹子/ 國際筆友夾子 [International Pen Pal Folders]. Participating teachers create folders on Google Drive for their learners to exchange letters with other learners in different Chinese programs, likely in different countries.

I hope to convey to my reader-teachers by presenting these successful collaborative projects that many bold ideas that might otherwise be unconceivable for one isolated local Chinese teacher are actually achievable through online communities and networks that transcend the geological constraint. We no longer need to compromise and restrain our creativity and imagination because at this point in history, where communication technology brings us closer than ever, someone may just respond and join us if we dare to put our wildest ideas out there.

Keep peace of mind

The last important note I would like to make to my fellow Chinese teachers is about the importance of keeping peace of mind while exploring new technology. Why is it so important to keep peace of mind and why does it seem so difficult when you begin your search for instructional technologies to implement in your teaching? One simple answer may be that there are just too many to choose from. In May 2017, the total number of iOS apps was over two million, and this number does not include apps in Windows or Android systems, independent software, and web-based services. It is very easy to look at all the choices we have to hand and feel utterly overwhelmed and lost. Therefore, *technology anxiety* is not uncommon among teachers across levels and subjects (Yaghi & Abu-Saba, 1998; Chou, 2003; Celik & Yesilyurt, 2013). To overcome technology anxiety and reach peace of mind when integrating technology into their design of learning, I would recommend teachers to remind themselves:

1.   Nobody knows everything, or nothing, about technology.

I consider myself as a capable and knowledgeable teacher when it comes to instructional technology, but I still see/hear of something new in this field almost on a daily basis. To know and learn every single new technology is a goal that is simply not humanly possible. Therefore, the utmost important thing I would like you to keep in mind is that it is completely normal and fine to have no idea what it is when someone mentions some technology. There is no need to beat yourself up. "Oh? Tell me more about it" is my usual reaction when this happens.

The other side of the concept "nobody knows everything about technology" is equally true and important: nobody knows *nothing* about technology. Let's put the pedagogical purpose aside and take a minute to think about the technologies you might already use in your daily life. Do you use email to correspond with others? Do you use Google Drive or Dropbox to share documents? Do you use Facebook? Twitter? Instagram? Do you use smart phones and their convenient apps? Do you Skype with your family or friends? Do you write, read, or comment on blogs? Do you watch YouTube videos? We live in such a time of human history that unless we make a conscious and extraordinary effort to avoid it, we use technology every single day. Therefore, I would encourage my fellow teachers who have experienced technology anxiety or any sense of inadequacy on this matter to change the mindset from "I know nothing about (certain) technology" to "I already know enough to start doing something with (certain) technology in my own teaching." This shift would allow us to see through the misconceived barrier of perceived technological competence and begin to realize the many possibilities we can already explore without stepping out of our comfort zone, which will bring us to the next reminder: Apply $i+1$ to yourself.

2.   Apply $i+1$ to yourself.

As established above, when it comes to technology, nobody knows everything and also nobody knows nothing. Therefore, when it comes to integrating technology into one's design of teaching and learning, we are not talking about leaping into a completely unknown realm. Instead, we expand on our prior knowledge and reach for what we are able to comprehend. For instance, many of us have already used PowerPoint in our daily instruction; a learnable next step may be to explore the functions that we have never used before, such as using the voice recording function to make your lecture a video, or making quiz games using the PowerPoint templates introduced earlier in this chapter; if you have used Google Docs to share materials with your class, you may consider social reading, peer editing, or collaborative writing using the same platform, all of which were introduced in Chapter 5; if you have started having learners watch instructional videos on YouTube, embedding interactive exercises or quizzes in the videos to check comprehension, as introduced in Chapter 6, might be the next function you want to add to it. The key is to fairly evaluate your current competence and comfort level (*i*) and explore just one step further within your range of learnability (+1). When conducting such self-assessment, please keep in mind the next reminder: You know what you and your learners need more than anyone else.

3.   You know what you and your learners need more than anyone else.

As mentioned in Chapter 2, a teacher's choice in regard to technology must be driven by their understanding of their learners and their design of the learning experience. This process is in fact highly individualized and based on the teacher's own need analysis. In other words, we do not use one technology simply because it is popular or recommended by other professionals. Although we might indeed learn from their experiences and insights, ultimately the learning experience in our classes is not about *them*. The choices and decisions should serve *me* and my learners' needs.

I sometimes call this need-driven process to find appropriate technologies "making wishes." One teacher's wishes may be different from another's. Naturally, different wishes would then require different technological tools or methods for their realization. For instance, some "wishes" I have personally made in the past decade include:

- I wished for a platform that allowed my students to easily record and post speech videos, as well as respond to each other also with speech videos. This wish led me to the discovery of Flipgrid (introduced in Chapter 4).
- I wished for more brainstorming and sharing among learners in the classroom and I ended up using Padlet (introduced in Chapter 4) to collect learners' thoughts synchronously and project them on the screen to prompt discussion.
- I wished to move instructive lectures out of the classroom so I could devote more class time to communicative projects, which was why I started implementing flipped learning in my classes (introduced in Chapter 6).

I have also witnessed other teachers' innovative use of technologies to realize their wishes, such as using Google Earth to explore a city in China, or creating a kinesthetic learning experience with 3-D printed models of turtle plastrons bearing oracle bone script [甲骨文] (see Figure 7.14). Even after many years of practicing and training teachers to use instructional technology, I am still constantly fascinated and inspired by the level of creativity and versatility these language teachers display in their designs.

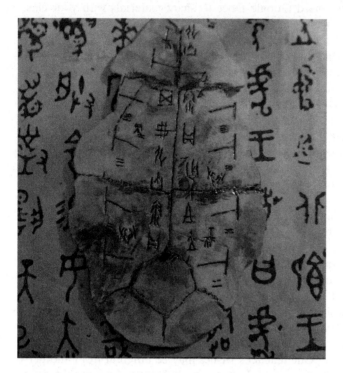

Figure 7.14 3-D model of a turtle plastron bearing oracle bone script
(Contributor: Yu-shan Cheng, Boston University)

After a teacher has identified their needs and made their wishes, the
question to follow is *how* these wishes are realized and become our instructional reality, which takes us to the next important thing I would like every
teacher to keep in mind: You are not alone.

4.   You are not alone.

As mentioned earlier in the section on teacher sharing and collaboration, there
are personal venues of master teachers one may follow, and online communities to join if you feel like connecting to other Chinese teachers in the field. In
addition to the aforementioned platforms, I also follow a few other e-journals,
blogs, and social media accounts pertaining to (instructional) technology,
such as: Practical Ed Tech (http://practicaledtech.com), Free Technology for
Teachers (www.freetech4teachers.com), and 全球话e视野—华语文数位教学/
全球話e視野—華語文數位教學 (www.facebook.com/ehuayu/). One subscription may lead you to more since it is quite common for bloggers and
social media users to repost one another with references.

　　These online community resources help us keep up with emerging technologies and tools from the user-practitioner's perspective. For more scholarly

inquiries, or empirical research about the learning impact of (certain) technology in light of pedagogical and linguistic theories, we may resort to academic journals or conferences, such as *CALICO* (the Computer-Assisted Language Instruction Consortium), *CALL* (Computer Assisted Language Learning), or *Language Learning & Technology*.

Major conferences focusing on foreign language education, such as ACTFL (American Council on the Teaching of Foreign Languages) and ECLL (the European Conference on Language Learning), or Chinese-specific conferences, such as CLTA (Chinese Language Teachers Association), NCLC (National Chinese Language Conference), or Chinese Language Association of Secondary-Elementary Schools (CLASS), often have sessions on technology-enhanced teaching and learning. Information about workshops and webinars on certain topics may also be found from their websites or listserv. In addition to acquiring knowledge and skills, another important function of such meetings is for teachers to meet, network, and collaborate with other teachers during and after the event.

Last but not least, one may always use a key word search on search engines or product forums to find technological solutions, as demonstrated in the case of video filming and editing tools in Chapter 6. An obvious advantage of using search engines to find tools is their prompt return of a wide array of options, while the biggest disadvantage is that these options are often less filtered and thus may require more testing by the teacher themselves to find the best fit. As I already stated in Chapter 6, it would be easier to receive more relevant results if one provides more specific information in the search box.

5. Do more with less.

Although technology brings many cognitive and affective benefits to learning, studies have warned us that attempting to incorporate (too much) technology without appropriate training and support may overwhelm teachers and learners alike (Hara, 2000; Lam, 2000; Young, 2004; Wood et al., 2005; Kessler, 2007; Schmid, 2008). A series of studies on learners' readiness to learn in a technology-enriched environment showed that despite their possession of basic technical, cognitive, and social skills required from daily life, such skills are not automatically carried over into a learning context. Appropriate pacing and scaffolding are necessary to help learners to strategically and sophisticatedly use technology to optimize learning (Hubbard, 2004; Winke & Goertler, 2008; Lai & Gu, 2011; Lai & Morrison, 2013). In other words, we should not overwhelm ourselves and our learners with too much learning on the technical side. Instead, allow yourself and your learners enough time and support to explore new technologies at a reasonable pace.

What pace is a reasonable pace? It differs among teachers, and the learners they have. One rule of thumb is that, as I stressed earlier, you should definitely NOT try to implement every single technology you encounter or are recommended. I personally explore and test hundreds of new tools and services every year, but do I implement all of them in my classes? Absolutely not. I use *at most* five to six technologies with any given group of learners in one semester, and the selection of tools differs according to learners' proficiency levels, learning objectives, and learning styles. I would rather keep the demand of learning new technologies low for my learners but use these technologies more frequently to fully exploit their impacts on learning.

So if we only choose five to six tools to use with a given group of learners, how do we make the decision among the many technologies available to us? This brings us back to the *filters* I laid out back in Chapter 2: Know your learners, focus on the design, and apply best-practice standards when selecting the tool. I would recommend prioritizing technologies that will significantly impact the curriculum and transform learning experiences (i.e., towards the "R" end of the SAMR model) over those that simply duplicate similar learning experiences with no additional learning benefits (i.e., towards the "S" end of the SAMR model).

Studies have shown that teachers' beliefs and attitudes are the most significant factors for technology integration into their curriculum and day-to-day instruction (Sugar, Crawley, & Fine, 2004; Hermans, Tondeur, van Braak, & Valcke, 2008; Teo, 2012). In other words, a teacher's mindset has more impact on their use of instructional technology than the external support (e.g., funding or technical support) and the actual experience/competence[8] with technology. Therefore, although many technological tools and techniques have been mentioned and discussed in this book and it would be to my delight if my readers try to use them in their own classes, the most powerful "tool" I would like my readers to realize they already have is their mind. The technical side of using instructional technology may change quickly because new tools are being developed by the second. However, a mindset that is confident because you already know enough to start, that is open to change and innovative ideas, that is assured because you know what you and your learners need, that is at peace because you give yourself time and opportunity to explore and receive support from the community, will help you thrive in this challenging yet immensely rewarding pursuit.

Resources

1.　Learning management systems:
　　Blackboard: www.blackboard.com/index.html
　　D2L: www.d2l.com
　　Moodle: https://moodle.com
　　Canvas: https://canvas.instructure.com/
　　Edmodo: www.edmodo.com
　　Schoology: www.schoology.com
　　Absorb: www.absorblms.com
　　Google Classroom: https://classroom.google.com/

2. Gamified learning management systems:
   ClassDojo: www.classdojo.com
   Class123: https://class123.ac
   Academy: www.growthengineering.co.uk/academy-lms/
   Edmodo: www.edmodo.com
   Classcraft: www.classcraft.com
3. Self-learning game apps:
   Duolingo: www.duolingo.com
   Microsoft Learning Chinese (iOS): https://itunes.apple.com/us/app/microsoft-learn-chinese/id1312951936?mt=8
   Fun Chinese: http://studycat.net/apps/fun-chinese/
   Word Swing Chinese: https://wordswing.com/
4. Some Chinese teachers' personal sharing venues:
   Practical Chinese: https://communicateinchinese.com
   Learn Chinese Teach Chinese: http://francesfu.blogspot.com
   Yi Lee's Mandarin Teaching Center: www.facebook.com/AlohaMandarin/
   Ignite Language: http://tprsforchinese.blogspot.com
5. Some e-Communities for teachers:
   On Facebook (accessible via a keyword search on www.facebook.com):
   CLTA 中文电影兴趣小组/中文電影興趣小組
   国际汉语教师—线上备课社团/國際漢語教師—線上備課社團
   中文教学百宝箱/中文教學百寶箱
   K-12 Chinese teachers' discussion group
   Mandarin Chinese Teachers in the UK
   On WeChat (accessible via members' invitation):
   国际汉语教师500强/國際漢語教師500強
   继承语教学工作室/繼承語教學工作室
   跨学科汉语教学/跨學科漢語教學
6. Information sites on instructional technologies:
   Practical Ed Tech: http://practicaledtech.com
   Free Technology for Teachers: www.freetech4teachers.com
   全球话e视野—华语文数位教学/全球話e視野—華語文數位教學: www.facebook.com/ehuayu/
7. Academic journals on instructional technologies for language teachers:
   CALICO (the Computer-Assisted Language Instruction Consortium): https://calico.org
   CALL (Computer Assisted Language Learning): www.tandfonline.com/toc/ncal20/current
   Language Learning & Technology: www.lltjournal.org/
8. Conferences that often have sessions for instructional technologies:
   ACTFL (American Council on the Teaching of Foreign Languages): www.actfl.org
   ECLL (the European Conference on Language Learning): https://ecll.iafor.org
   CLTA (Chinese Language Teachers Association): http://clta-us.org

NCLC (National Chinese Language Conference): https://asiasociety.org/national-chinese-language-conference

CLASS (Chinese Language Association of Secondary-Elementary Schools): www.classk12.org

CALICO (the Computer-Assisted Language Instruction Consortium): https://calico.org

Tools

1. Tools for interactive assignments:

Product Name	Liveworksheets
Function	Create online interactive worksheets
Difficulty Level	★
Product Website	www.liveworksheets.com

Product Name	Tinytap (mobile app)
Function	Create interactive flipbook style exercises
Difficulty Level	★
Product Website	www.tinytap.it

Product Name	Classkick
Function	Create online exercises for individual or group assignments
Difficulty Level	★
Product Website	www.classkick.com

2. Quiz game tools:

Product Name	PowerPoint
Function	Create guessing, matching, and jeopardy games
Difficulty Level	★
Product Website	www.microsoft.com/en-us/store/b/powerpoint-2016 Jeopardy template: https://templates.office.com/en-us/Education

Product Name	Kahoot
Function	Create interactive quiz games
Difficulty Level	☆
Product Website	https://kahoot.com/

Product Name	Quizizz
Function	Create interactive quiz games
Difficulty Level	☆
Product Website	https://quizizz.com

Product Name	Quizlet Live
Function	Create interactive quiz games
Difficulty Level	☆
Product Website	https://quizlet.com/

Notes

1 CourseSites is a free alternative to Blackboard developed by the same company.
2 Online flipbook refers to the interactive format that provides an experience similar to flipping pages of a printed document. Most e-book services adopt this technique by allowing users to tap the edge of a page, swipe it left and right, or click on an arrow icon.
3 Liveworksheets.com has limited options for teacher comments after submission.
4 The players' names are entered by learners at the beginning of the game, which do not have to be their real names.
5 Unlike normal Kahoot games that can be played on any browser, Kahoot Challenges may only be played in its mobile app (both iOS and Android).
6 According to Duolingo (http://making.duolingo.com/say-nihao-to-duolingos-chinese-course), the current course content also covers half of the content of Level 4 of HSK.
7 The paid tiers of Classcraft allows for more gaming and class management options, including more career classes for the characters.
8 Teachers' "perceived" competence with technology on the other hand has a significant impact on their adoption of technology, as an attitudinal factor.

References

Buckingham, J. (2014). Open digital badges for the uninitiated. *The Electronic Journal for English as a Second Language, 18*(1), 1–11.

Caponetto, I., Earp, J., & Ott, M. (2014, October). Gamification and education: A literature review. In *European Conference on Games Based Learning* (Vol. 1; pp. 50–57). Reading, UK: Academic Conferences International Limited.

Celik, V., & Yesilyurt, E. (2013). Attitudes to technology, perceived computer self-efficacy and computer anxiety as predictors of computer supported education. *Computers & Education, 60*(1), 148–158.

Chou, C. (2003). Incidences and correlates of Internet anxiety among high school teachers in Taiwan. *Computers in Human Behavior, 19*(6), 731–749.

Fenton, W. (2018, January). The best (LMS) learning management systems for 2018. *PC Magazine.* Retrieved from www.pcmag.com/article2/0,2817,2488347,00.asp

Flores, J. F. F. (2015). Using gamification to enhance second language learning. *Digital Education Review, 27*, 32–54.

Hara, N. (2000). Student distress in a web-based distance education course. *Information, Communication & Society, 3*(4), 557–579.

Hermans, R., Tondeur, J., van Braak, J., & Valcke, M. (2008). The impact of primary school teachers' educational beliefs on the classroom use of computers. *Computers & Education, 51*(4), 1499–1509.

Hubbard, P. (2004). Learner training for effective use of CALL. In S. Fotos & C. M. Browne (Eds.), *New perspectives on CALL for second language classrooms* (pp. 45–68). Mahwah, NJ: Lawrence Erlbaum Associates.

Ingwersen, H. (2018, January 24). *6 gamified learning management systems compared* [Blog post]. Retrieved from https://blog.capterra.com/6-gamified-lmss-compared/

Kapp, K. M. (2012). *The gamification of learning and instruction: Game-based methods and strategies for training and education.* Hoboken, NJ: John Wiley & Sons.

Kessler, G. (2007). Formal and informal CALL preparation and teacher attitude toward technology. *Computer Assisted Language Learning, 20*(2), 173–188.

Lai, C., & Gu, M. Y. (2011). Self-regulated out-of-class language learning with technology. *Computer Assisted Language Learning, 24*, 317–335.

Lai, C., & Morrison, B. (2013). Towards an agenda for learner preparation in technology-enhanced language learning environments. *CALICO Journal, 30*(2), 154–162.

Lam, Y. (2000). Technophilia vs. technophobia: A preliminary look at why second-language teachers do or do not use technology in their classrooms. *Canadian Modern Language Review, 56*(3), 389–420.

Liu, Y. J. (Ed.). (2016). *Authentic materials for Chinese teaching and learning*. Retrieved from www.teach-chinese.com/download/

Liu, Y. J. (Ed.). (2018). *Understanding China through video clips*. Retrieved from www.teach-chinese.com/download/

New Media Consortium. (2014). *Horizon report on technology and higher education*. Retrieved from: www.nmc.org/publication/nmc-horizon-report-2014-higher education-edition/

Schmid, E. C. (2008). Potential pedagogical benefits and drawbacks of multimedia use in the English language classroom equipped with interactive whiteboard technology. *Computers & Education, 51*(4), 1553–1568.

Sugar, W., Crawley, F., & Fine, B. (2004). Examining teachers' decisions to adopt new technology. *Journal of Educational Technology & Society, 7*(4), 201–213.

Teo, T. (2012). Examining the intention to use technology among pre-service teachers: An integration of the technology acceptance model and theory of planned behavior. *Interactive Learning Environments, 20*(1), 3–18.

Werbach, K., & Hunter, D. (2012). *For the win: How game thinking can revolutionize your business*. Philadelphia, PA: Wharton Digital Press.

Winke, P., & Goertler, S. (2008). Did we forget someone? Students' computer access and literacy for CALL. *CALICO Journal, 25*(3), 482–509.

Wood, E., Mueller, J., Willoughby, T., Specht, J., & Deyoung, T. (2005). Teachers' perceptions: Barriers and supports to using technology in the classroom. *Education, Communication & Information, 5*(2), 183–206.

Yaghi, H. M., & Abu-Saba, M. B. (1998). Teachers' computer anxiety: An international perspective. *Computers in Human Behavior, 14*(2), 321–336.

Young, J. (2004). When good technology means bad teaching: Giving professors gadgets without training can do more harm than good in the classroom, students say. *The Chronicle of Higher Education, 51*(12), A31–A37.

Index